Diary of a
SHANGHAI
SHOWGIRL

Raising the Red Curtain
on China...Uncensored

by
Amelia Kallman

Beaux Press

Published by Beaux Press 2015

ISBN-13:
978-1514605950

ISBN-10:
1514605953

www.diaryofashanghaishowgirl.com

For Norman

CONTENTS

ACKNOWLEDGEMENTS

Cover by Norman Gosney
Cover photos by Robert Sedo
Sedo Photography
www.sedophotography.com

To view photos that correlate to chapters in this book,
Please visit
www.diaryofashanghaishowgirl.com

PROLOGUE

"If they separate us, don't say anything."

Compulsively, I checked my pocket again for the numbers of my embassy and lawyers, my veins pulsing as if I'd chugged ten cups of coffee, my eyes wide with paranoia behind sunglasses. Pudong airport was crowded. Standing there in line, I was hyper aware that the military Chinese security guards surrounded us from a distance. I felt their shifty eyes on my back, as if they might close in at any second. Trying to focus on breathing, I reminded myself that it's easy. In, out, in, then... I could feel my terror radiating, threatening to swallow me whole.

So far things were going to plan, but it wasn't over yet. This was the final test. Silently I prayed to God, Jah, Muhammad, Krishna, Buddha, Stevie Wonder, anyone who'd listen really, hoping that there wasn't a warrant issued for our arrest or a WANTED poster on the other side of that counter.

It was crazy to think that just eight hours ago I put these fears behind me long enough to kick one last Can Can at my nightclub, CHINATOWN. It's true what they say: The show must go on. Basking in the standing ovation of a packed Friday night house, I took my final curtain call before saying teary goodbyes to our cast, employees, and friends. It already felt like years ago.

I didn't want to leave. Shanghai was my home, my life. Behind the anxiety, and seething anger, I was already mourning the life I was leaving behind. I glanced at our baggage: Two lonely suitcases. The same ones we arrived with three years earlier.

The Chinese couple in front of us got their tickets. A pang of envy hit me as they walked towards their gate. We were up. I squeezed Norman's hand tight. We were in this thing together. The woman behind the counter sat stiffly. She had a burgundy scarf in a tight knot around her neck and black hair pulled up into a snood. As we approached, her lips didn't move to form a smile or say hello, she just stared at us through glasses that kept slipping down her flat, oily nose reflecting the fluorescent lights. Handing her our passports, we forced polite smiles. She took them and typed into the computer. We stood there, trying to act casual. The longest minutes of my life.

Rising sharply she said, "Excuse me, please wait here," and marched towards the back office, clutching our passports in front of her chest.

I thought I was going to be sick.

PART 1:

CHINA 101

CHAPTER 1 – What have I done?

We lost a whole day and woke up in the future. I was standing in China on a dare. My eyes scanned the Pudong International Airport for a breath of familiarity. The white walls and armed soldiers let me know that I wasn't in New York anymore. I held my breath as Norman grabbed my hand, resuscitating me. One look into his brown eyes and I came back down to earth again. It was 2007 and I just turned twenty-three.

Norman's friend, Tino, was supposed to meet us there. It was Tino who first said that we should move to Shanghai and open a nightclub there. Norman and Tino worked together back in New York. Not in an office or anything. They were part of a small, boutique enterprise that may or may not have sold the world's finest marijuana to the rich and famous. Shortly before we decided to leave New York, one of the deliveries went missing and there were rumors that someone had talked. Small businesses can be tricky like that.

We waited at the airport for an hour and a half,

but Tino never showed. Finding Wifi, Norman got word that 'work was piling up' and Tino had to postpone his trip, which was taken as code for shit's hit the fan and he couldn't leave the country. Norman never talked to me about that business, probably to protect me, but I knew that Tino was a front man for a larger organization. 'Close associates', he called them. While these guys often came in handy when it comes to financing nightclubs, I was smart enough to know that the less I knew about such close associates, the better.

"Don't worry," Norman said with a smile, assuring me that this was an adventure and everything was going to be fine. And of course, I believed him.

In New York, Norman and I had a business together too. We ran a totally illegal burlesque speakeasy, The Blushing Diamond, on the 10th floor of a windowless office building on 29th Street between 6th and Broadway. The secret club became the nightspot of choice for Manhattan's most elite - and discreet - celebrity and bohemian cliental. At the shows, aptly named Guilty Pleasures, Norman acted as emcee, I was his showgirl assistant, and we had a six-girl, singing and dancing chorus line made up of the best burlesque artists in the world. They performed alongside Freddy Fontaine, our Sinatra-singing star, and several male character actors called 1st and 2nd Bananas. It required a password to enter and we only sold high-end bottles of chilled Champagne, and branded hipflasks of whiskey and vodka. The Blushing Diamond was massively successful, attracting the likes of Björk and Matthew Barney, Robert De Niro, Wes Anderson and Woody Harrelson, to name a few. Every night we opened, we rammed our jewel box theatre, relying solely on word-of-mouth and the ever-escalating rumors of our forbidden delights.

When a brothel opened up next door, the police started to stakeout the street and we got a tip-off that the speakeasy was going to be raided. I helped Norman pack it all up and we moved out in the middle of the night. When the cops finally came they found nothing but an empty rehearsal space.

At the time, Norman was always talking about the looming economic crisis, and Tino, who did a lot of work in the rag-trade in China, kept saying that Shanghai was the place to be. They seemed to agree that the Chinese were on the brink of becoming the next superpower. Norman designed and opened nightclubs all over the world: Tokyo, Moscow, Munich, Thailand and Belize, but China had always been out of the question. Until now. Asia was the last untapped market and if he got in now and opened one of his signature nightclubs, he reasoned he could own the brand of burlesque in China, and would open a chain of cabaret nightclubs across Asia, standing to make a fortune. Norman has always been an icebreaker, discovering new cultural phenomenon and making them cool, but then the cruise ships, or big business, would eventually catch up and come through to reap the benefits. In China, Norman intended to be the cruise ship.

The night we packed up the speakeasy, we contemplated what to do next. We were at the top of our game, in the world's top city. Where do we go from here? Then I blurted out that he should get Tino's friends to put up the money for a nightclub in China. What was he waiting for? He said if he did go that I'd have to come with him to help run the shows.

"Of course," I said without blinking.

Silent minutes followed and in that silence we found ourselves agreeing to move to China. Norman sold his shares in the boutique enterprise, and leased his penthouse apartment atop the legendary Chelsea Hotel, giving us nearly a million to position us in China, invest in our Shanghai nightclub, and get the ball rolling.

We collected our two suitcases and took a cab into the city of Shanghai. Riding with heads out the windows like over-excited dogs, we passed flat yellow fields with the occasional patch of tall, beige, derelict buildings appearing out of nowhere, and disappearing just as fast like eerie ghost towns. I started to get worried. Was this it?

Penetrating deeper, the city finally began to appear, like Gotham City, or something out of *Blade Runner*. An extraordinary amount of dull, browning, high-rise apartment towers lined the hazy horizon, each with enclosed balconies and the day's washing flapping in the wind. For a brand new city built in
the last fifteen years or so, the inconsistencies in architecture and standards were puzzling. It ranged from impressive, post-modernist towers, to structures that looked like they were trying way too hard, coming across as tacky and sadly passé. Another thing that jumped out was all the orange uniformed construction workers climbing on bamboo scaffolding like jungle gyms surrounding the city, up so high they were above the birds. Vertigo washed over me just looking at them. And then of course, the amount of people. I'd never seen such a mass density of people. They were everywhere I looked.

"The most populous city in the world," Norman said. "A city of over twenty-two million, my love."

"Twenty-two million and two," I corrected him with a kiss on the cheek, trying hard to believe that I made the right decision leaving everything behind and moving to China.

At the Howard Johnson's All-Suites Hotel we crashed hard after scarfing down dumplings from room service. At two-thirty in the morning I woke up in a frantic sweat, forgetting where I was, and then remembering, feeling displaced and strangely emotional, like I could cry. It was the same deep emptiness I felt that time I got lost in the supermarket when I was four. I wanted my mom. My eyes pinned open. Little lights flickered around their edges as if an unfamiliar drug had spiked me.

Jetlag.

Norman was awake too. Television offered little comfort besides a brief, morbid fascination with - not one, but two - Filipino channels devoted strictly to cock-fighting. I'd never seen anything as graphic as the commercials for steroids, cocks and sperm.

"Unless you count Christopher Street in the West Village," Norman teased. Somehow he still managed to make me laugh.

We fell back to sleep around seven a.m. and abruptly woke up that afternoon, both of us sick as dogs. Full on vomiting and diarrhea, our bodies natural reaction to the air on that side of the planet, the muddy smog of pollution that engulfed the city, and maybe the food from the night before. For several days we didn't leave the room, took turns visiting the lavatory and kept our distance, as there was nothing romantic about the way we looked or smelled.

And just when I thought it couldn't get any worse, a typhoon came streaming across the city sending our suite on the 30th floor swaying back and forth in the gusting wind. Lying wide-awake on my side of the bed, staring at the ceiling fan, trying not to throw up, there was only one thought running through my mind:

What have I done?

CHAPTER 2 – Smelly Tofu

Before we left New York, I went to a party where a friend of a friend scribbled a number on the back of a gum wrapper of someone she knew who lived in Shanghai. Gage +86 2152923645 was the only person we sorta kinda knew in that hemisphere now that Tino had been held up.

I took a chance and called the gum wrapper guy. Gage agreed to meet us for dinner. The taxi was only fourteen 'kwai'. RMB or Yuan are the official names for Chinese currency, but locals call it kwai, meaning pieces. The exchange rate was about seven kwai to the dollar. Really cheap. I asked Norman why there's still a portrait of Chairman Mao on the money, even though he was responsible for the mass genocide of his own people? For once, he didn't have the answer. To be honest, until about four weeks earlier I couldn't have pointed to Shanghai on a map. In the weeks leading up to leaving, I'd done my best to bone up on China. I knew that it was a Communist country, that they could only have one child, and that just about everything I owned was made there. Then I read on the internet somewhere that Mao had killed more people than Hitler and Stalin combined. Combined! And it happened relatively recently too. I decided to stop reading after that.

A blinking red and yellow neon sign of vertical Chinese characters flashed over the restaurant door. Beneath it read 'Noble Food'. Who knew food could be noble? Inside I watched the waitresses bustle across the floor like I was watching a National Geographic special. Like I had never seen a Chinese person up close before. My brain went into a whispered narration as they plodded from table to table in their Chinese dresses, shoulders hunched, pushing glasses up noses and standing very close to their customers.

It occurred to me that I didn't have a phone and forgot to tell Gage what we looked like. I glanced at Norman, standing there in a gray and pink pinstripe, three-piece suit, handsome and slim. He may have been in his mid-fifties, but he looked ten years younger, with more energy than guys half his age. He recently got his full head of salt-and-pepper hair cut into a quasi-Mohawk, shaved on the sides with a quiff at the front. It suited him. And me, feeling slightly overdressed in a little black dress that hugged my tall, feminine curves, high-heels, and my long, reddish-brown hair dangling below my shoulders, framing my voluptuous chest.

And then I looked around. Every other person in the room had black hair, tan skin and brown eyes. We stood out like cockroaches on a wedding cake.

Gage spotted us right away. Half Chinese, half Australian, he looked exotic, like a male model with chiseled cheekbones and a hard jaw line. With bed-head black hair, he looked like a rocker in skinny black jeans, Doc Martins and a Motorhead t-shirt. Flashing us a killer, good-teeth smile, I found him instantly likable and had a feeling we were going to be friends.

"How ya guys feeling?" he asked in a thick Aussie accent.

"Good, good! Happy to be alive. We're getting over jetlag and a bit of a stomach thing too, but I think the worst is over," said Norman.

"Ah, don't be so sure mate. You guys just passing through or here for good?"

"Here for bad," I piped in with a smirk.

As we took our seats around a circular table, Gage told us that he'd been in Shanghai just over a year. He said he worked for the devil, eventually clarifying that he meant he worked in advertising. I asked how he liked Shanghai. He hesitated a second before answering.

"Yeah, it's good, I like it a lot. It's definitely having a moment right now. You've picked a really good time to come."

Norman and I exchanged a pleased look.

"It's like the Wild West out here. Like living on the edge of the world. There's so much going on all the time. I love that. But it can be hard sometimes too, I can't lie. I mean, 'This is China'. I have a love-hate thing-"

He paused and changed the subject.

"So this is Sichuan food, which is a bit spicy and zestier than some other kinds, but I think it's the best."

In traditional Chinese fashion, he explained, the person who invited the others to dinner is the one who orders the food for everyone to share family-style and at the end, the inviter is expected to pay for it all too. He added that we had to try everything or else it would be considered rude. Gage said this with a suspicious glint in his eye so I braced myself. Bring on the noble food!

Dishes started coming out in no particular order as soon as we ordered. Some of it was sensational, like the dumplings, fried rice, and spicy aubergines in soy sauce. Other dishes? Not so much. None of it was like any Chinese food I'd ever eaten before. There was no Kung Pow Chicken anywhere in sight. The dishes kept coming, everything from yummy pork ribs and scrumptious crispy duck, to surprisingly tasty jellyfish and some unrecognizable gelatinous balls. Gage chuckled watching me try to maneuver them with chopsticks before I gave up and stabbed the little suckers triumphantly. Then a smell as bad as the ape house at the zoo on a hot summer's day ran up my nose tripping my gag reflex. I covered my nose with my hand, noticing there weren't any napkins about.

"I can't believe you just did that at the table," I whispered to Norman in offense.

"Me? I thought it was you!"

Then our eyes turned to the table as it dawned on us that the smell was coming from the latest food to arrive. Food that Gage was scooping into his mouth, anticipating our reaction.

"What *is* that?" I said, thinking I might be ill. It smelled like a sewer. Worse than a sewer.

"Smelly Tofu. That's what it's called. Bù yào ma? You don't want?"

"Boo-Yea-ow- Ma!" I said, doing my best to make it clear that I most definitely did not want *that* anywhere near my mouth.

Gage laughed so hard at my disgusted face and bad pronunciation that beer went up his nose. Catching his breath he explained, the 'Ma' part was only used when asking a question, but 'Bù yào' means 'don't want'. I repeated it, happy to learn my first phrase in Mandarin. Looks like it would prove a useful one at that.

After I finished eating, I excused myself to the restroom. As the door swung open, thick, syrupy incense wafted over me, followed seconds later by the smell of urine. I opened a stall door and froze at what I saw: The dreaded squat toilet. I'd read about these. Just a hole in the ground basically. I wasn't even sure which direction I was supposed to face? Contemplating holding it, I told myself I didn't have to go that bad. But that was a lie. I did have to go that bad. Anyways, that kind of attitude wasn't going to get me anywhere, I reminded myself. This is China and I am fully committed. Fully committed. I'd have to get used to it sooner or later. Luckily, I had been a Girl Scout in my past life and am less precious than I sometimes let on, so I pinched my nose and got on with it.

Of course, there wasn't any toilet paper then. It wasn't even like they ran out. They just don't supply it in public toilets. Awesome. And, to top it off, there was no soap either. Geez Louise.

Norman has a joke that the bathrooms of Chinese restaurants have signs that say, 'Employees must wash hands before returning to Wok'.

Yeah. Not so funny anymore.

CHAPTER 3 – Burlesque Comes to China

Exploring the streets of Shanghai at night for the first time, we took a taxi headed to a lounge. An extraordinary city, saturated with buildings covered in blinking, sparkling, changing-color lights, animating like early video games. Blinding LED screens pop up every ten meters showing commercials of Western teenage models in bras and panties. In the back of the cabs are screens too, showing commercials of pale Chinese girls advertising face bleaching creams and armpit bleaching deodorant, and one of some poor bloke who relieves his bad stomach inside a sandcastle on a beach. We turned onto the main highway that cuts through town, the Yan'an Lu, which has a high road and a low road. Both completely lit-up in blue neon. The electricity bill of this city must be unreal.

"Bringing burlesque to China? Ha!" Gage clapped. "I love it. That is just what this city needs."

He asked Norman if he knew that he needed to have a Chinese partner to open a business here. He explained that one was necessary due to 'Guangxi'.

"It means influence. Who you know, or how well-connected you are to The Party."

Norman told him about the Chinese billionaire movie producer Tino had interested in investing, along with of course, Tino's close associates, who had also expressed interest. Gage proceeded to tell us several horror stories about Chinese partners pulling the rug out from under their 'lǎowài' partners.

He turned around from the front seat to face us.

"One day the foreign partner shows up for work and the office isn't there any more. The phone numbers have changed, and if you take them to court, contract in hand, you'll lose every time because they're Chinese and you're not."

"So how do you get the gwang-she without the Chinese partner?" I wanted to know.

"That's a good question. You can't really. It's kind of a catch twenty-two. You just gotta hope you make the right choice in partners and pray for the best."

I looked at Norman, wondering what he thought about that. I was beginning to get the picture that doing business in China was going to be quite different from New York.

"Some people get their Ayi to be their Chinese partner."

"What's an I.E.?"

"You don't know what an Ayi is? You really have just gotten off the slow boat, haven't you? It's your maid, it's what you call her. You'll have one when you get settled. Everyone has one. I haven't made my bed, or done the washing up, or my own laundry in years."

'Ayi' actually translates to auntie, or 'woman over forty'. Try getting away with that in New York.

To make the night our official Shanghai introduction, Gage decided that we needed to see the Bund, Shanghai's most famous attraction. The Bund is an area on the Puxi side of the Pudong River, which separates Shanghai's two parts: Pudong, 'Commonly thought of as the boring, unstylish, business side', and Puxi, 'Where everything worth knowing about happens, and everyone worth knowing lives'.

The old buildings we walked by along the river previously housed the banks and embassies in the colonial 1920's and '30's when this was the hub of the Asian financial world. They were originally designed in the Cathedral of Commerce style to resemble the skyline of Liverpool, England, oddly enough. Across the river, in what had been potato fields twenty years earlier, was the new hub, the now famous skyline seen on the cover of Shanghai travel books. There stands one of the weirdest buildings in the world, simply called The Pudong Tower. To me, it looked like a spaceship of two, constantly color-changing, stacked balls, on either end of a gigantic, ironed atom, like mutated DNA, ready to launch into space. I'm told its purely decorative, designed to anchor the skyline in memory. Gage says there's an aquarium in one of the globes.

The Jin Mao Tower is next to it, decked in lavish gold lights. It's upstaged only by its close proximity to a huge, LED-screen projecting a continuous commercial of two parrots necking, advertising Fuji Film. Also extremely visible is the HSBC building, the Hong Kong & Shanghai Banking Corporation. Gage pointed out bamboo scaffolding reaching skywards ninety-stories in the air. Construction was underway on The World Financial Building, competing to be one of the tallest buildings in the world.

As I inhaled the night air coming off the river, I could feel in every cell of my body that I was on the other side of the planet from everything I'd ever known before. Here I had no past, only a future. I was free to reinvent myself into whoever I wanted to be. I felt like I could do anything.

CHAPTER 4 – Anything is Possible

We ducked into the Glamour Bar for cocktails. The lounge looked like the inside of a hooker's handbag. A 1980's hooker, that is. Plush, satin pinks and gold, diamond-shapes echoed throughout. Black leather couches, dripping crystal chandeliers, mirror top, coke-cutting tables. Gage said it had been there almost ten years. The first restaurant on the Bund, it was also one of the rare success stories of foreigner ownership.

Norman wandered off to take a look around the place. Gage and I ordered two Moscow Mules and a Ginger Ale for Norm, who doesn't drink. A lengthy pregnant pause followed after we placed our order, like on a first date when you kind of wiggle in your seat nervously, pretending to recognize the song playing or something, while brains scramble for an appropriate and casual-sounding topic of conversation. We were both about to say something when Gage broke the silence.

"So, you're, like, a stripper?"

Not what I expected him to say.

When I first started working with Norman when I was twenty-one, I was never sure how to respond to that question. The word 'stripper' has a lot of negative connotations that 'burlesque' somehow seems to escape, despite the fact that both professions pertain to the seductive removal of clothing for the entertainment and titillation of an audience.

There's an old joke:

Q: What's the difference between a stripper and a burlesque artist?

A: A stripper makes money.

Most burlesque artists are attracted to the often inconsistent and sporadic work because of the endless creative possibilities for self-expression. They see it as their art. But as with so many artistic fields, it's not an area you go into expecting to get rich.

I know most people's only reference point to burlesque is Dita von Teese in all her glassy, plastic, pin-up perfection, operating on a budget that is out of this world. Then of course, there is the other side of that with wannabe burlesquers who cringingly look like they're trying to work out their personal issues on stage.

I told all this to Gage, glad our drinks arrived. Then I attempted to explain that I'm not a stripper, or a burlesque artist really. I'm a showgirl. But not like Elizabeth Berkley or Gina Gershon in the movie, I'm a good old-fashioned, singing, dancing, acting, scantily-clad, cheeky showgirl.

It's a real profession, I swear.

When I first met Norman, I was an acting student, having worked as a professional child actress in New York and D.C. doing theatre, films and commercials. I didn't really know what the word 'burlesque' meant until I met him. When it came time to produce one of his famous variety shows though, I was resolute that I wanted to be involved. The truth was, I didn't like the idea of leaving my boyfriend alone at late night rehearsals with gorgeous women who were prone to taking their clothes off. So Norman told me to come up with a part for myself in the show, and that is the short story of how I became a showgirl.

On stage, I am Miss Amelia, a bubbly showgirl-next-door, self-assured and unafraid, who can't help but be the modest center of attention in dazzling, Vegas-style costumes of rhinestones, sequins and feathers. Showgirls are a bit like Western Geishas. We are actresses who sing, dance and use our provocative looks to draw attention to our talents. The ultimate tease, we combine skill, smarts and beauty, showing off enough to send pulses racing and imaginations soaring, but without giving the satisfaction of a full reveal.

"Anyways, enough about me. What about you? Do you have girlfriend?" I figured that he was too good-looking not to.

"I had one recently. An expat girl. But she's gone back to Canada now. People come and go from this city. It's hard for things to last," his voice trailed off and his eyes followed. For a second, I thought I'd hit a sore spot, but he snapped out of it stating, "Shanghai's where relationships come to die."

"Really?" I was taken aback. "Why do you say that?" I tried to control the defensiveness rising in my voice.

"A lot of women - wives, girlfriends - they don't like it here. I'm not saying it'll happen to you, but..." He stopped to get his words right, as if afraid that he might accidently reveal some kind of male conspiracy.

Then he just blurted it out.

"It's because all the girls here are really hot and skinny and they throw themselves at foreign guys. Even the unattractive nerds, bordering on Aspergic, who couldn't get laid in their own countries, here they get young, hot wives *and* mistresses."

Wow. I'd wondered what the girls here would be like. If they'd all be really sexy and perfect, and wondered if Norman would be attracted to them. But I figured these were private concerns, and certainly never expected it to be put out on the table so upfront.

"And because of how business gets done here," he added.

"Business? What do you mean 'business'?"

"I don't want to scare you."

It was too late.

"You can't say something like 'This is where relationships come to die', and then not explain what that means. Just tell me the truth. I can handle it."

At least, I hoped I could.

"See the Chinese love to drink with us. They think that by taking you out and getting you pissed up on Baijiu until you puke that they'll gain face and you'll think they're cool. Obviously. So you go out... and they aren't the best drinkers... they mix expensive red wine with things like Coca-Cola and Green Tea, and then take it like a shot, I kid you not. And then you have to go to KTV with them."

"Nice place," Norman said, startling me as he slid into the banquet by my side. "Sorry, what are you guys talking about?"

"I was about to tell Amelia what a KTV is. Do you know?" Norman shrugged. "Okay. KTV means karaoke. They love karaoke. I was just telling her that a lot of business deals get done here over large amounts of alcohol and trips to the KTV parlors, and that pisses off a lot of wives and girlfriends."

"I like karaoke," I said, on behalf of the whole female species. Salt & Peppa's 'Shoop-Shoop' came to the blurry cobwebs of my mind.

"A KTV is a brothel. Well, not always, there are legit ones too, but a lot of the time. You can tell though. And they want to buy you a girl." He said it like it was just a fact of life. "They insist."

"But isn't that illegal?" I protested. I mean we are in Communist China, right?

Gage cracked a half smile, sipped his drink, and said, "Shanghai has a slogan. It goes like this: There's a rule against everything, and anything is possible."

I repeated it back to him, making sure I memorized that. It's the *anything is possible* part that I liked.

He leaned in, "Anyways, the government runs the KTVs. The best ones, with the hottest girls, are for policemen and government officials only." He raised his black eyebrows earnestly and nodded, and then he remembered, "Oh, and massage parlors too."

Great. Wouldn't want to forget about the massage parlors.

"But see, look over there," he nodded in the direction of a middle-aged white guy. He was sat in a wrinkled suit, had a paunch belly, wore glasses and his graying hair was thinning on the top. He looked like one of my friend's fathers. He sat with his hands up the thigh of a young, lanky local girl with long, straight, jet-black hair who looked like she didn't speak much English.

"See. That's what they don't like."

Stopping off for one last drink, we arrived at his favorite dive bar, Logo. The street was full of kids. Hipsters holding beer cans, smoking cigarettes, eating kebabs. In front of the door a spiky-hair teenage boy flogged cigarettes. Gage told me the cigarettes were fakes, Western label on Chinese product. He asked if I smoke.

"I do. I mean, I did, but I've just quit."

"You've picked a bad place to come if you're trying to quit. You can smoke anywhere here. In taxis, clubs, supermarkets, elevators. Everyone smokes."

Just talking about it made me want a cigarette, but I was determined to keep my willpower. But after a few drinks it got harder.

"He also sells hashish and papers. Wanna smoke a joint?"

"What? Really? Are you serious?" He had to be messing with me. "Won't we get arrested?"

Gage smiled and cocked his head to his shoulder as if admiring a cute baby. Then I watched him walk over and do the deal. I couldn't believe it. Just like that? Impressive. Can't even do that in New York.

"The Chinese don't know what it is. The Uyghurs bring it in from Turkey."

As he began to roll, he explained that there are a hundred and fifty-six different ethnic groups in China with the Han Chinese at seventy percent, making up the majority.

"But the locals are more into hard drugs, like Special K. Don't assume lines on the table are coke, it's more likely K. Anyways," he licked the joint. "They don't really care what foreigners do, it's only if you're Chinese. I have to be more careful than most expats since I look Chinky, but my Mandarin's so bad they know pretty fast that I'm not from here. There's another place, called YY's on Nanchang Lu, Communist flag hanging outside. You can smoke openly there, like in Amsterdam."

Inspecting the hashish, Norman lit up like a Christmas tree.

Through the red paneled doors of the small club, I entered into a dim room covered in layers of international graffiti art. It had a seedy, underbelly edge to it, like you could get lost there, and looking around, I had the feeling that some of the kids already had. The beat up leather couches were crowded with chatting people around my age in various stages of inebriation. Mostly white faces speaking English. I never expected to feel so relieved to see faces and hear voices like mine. Some very black faces too, standing together next to the wall and checking me out as I followed Norm into the next room. Gage touched my hips and whispered in my ear.

"Nigerian coke dealers."

This town was chock full of surprises.

On the other side of velvet curtains was a backroom dive. The room was dark except for a string of Christmas lights and a television hung in the corner playing Jamaica's own, *The Harder They Come*. The deejay, who appeared to be a Chinese Rasta, was spinning the kids into a reggae-dubstep trance, arms in the air, vibing to the stiff beats. I took a puff of Gage's spliff, said a few 'Gān bēi's' clinking Tsingtao beer bottles with the guys, and then hit the dance floor, feeling tipsy and high and right at home.

Now I had a new thought that I couldn't get out of my brain:

Here, anything is possible.

CHAPTER 5 – New York Meets Shanghai

"He's here darling," Norman called out.

I smacked my glossed lips and took one last look in the mirror. Yeah, the red pumps and heart-shaped Lolita sunglasses were probably a bit much with my leggings and tank top, but screw it. Everyone stared at me anyways, the least I could do was look good.

It was another sun-drenched day with a light breeze, perfect for exploring new territories on a bike ride with Gage. A few weeks ago I was scared to death of riding a bicycle in these bustling streets, but soon it became second nature. I had to get in touch with my aggressive-driver side, but the payoff was worth it. Riding my bike was one of my favorite things to do now, and the best way to see the city. Bicycles and motorbikes have their own lanes and no one bothers wearing helmets. Bike theft is the most frequent and common crime in Shanghai. I know because I was already on bike number two.

Cars were only introduced to the city about ten years ago, making eighty-percent of people behind the wheel first-time drivers. There are approximately thirteen-hundred new cars on the streets of Shanghai every week. And they're all blowing their horns.

We moved into a second floor walk up, two-bedroom apartment on Fuxing Zhong Lu. It's a very fashionable, tree-lined street in the center of the French Concession. Our lime green apartment complex, Jubilee Court, was built in 1925 to house wealthy French magnates. Then it was requisitioned after the revolution for officials of The Communist Party. The court stretched from Fuxing Lu, the former Boulevard Liberte, to the Huaihai Lu, the former Avenue Foche.

The Art Deco style of irregular rectangles at irreverent angles, and ironwork of rigid diamonds and starbursts, made our building look like a Hollywood set for a fantasy Oriental adventure. Along with Mexico City, Shanghai has one of the largest Art Deco areas in the world, owed mostly to the French and European population of the late 1920's and early '30's. Imaginations ran wild in the city, resulting in some of the most extreme examples of Art Brutal and Deco ever seen. In the various national concessions, the architects of each nation were free to build unrestrained, fantasy versions of their mother country's style-de-jour. You got everything from elegant Art Nouveau mansions, to blocky Tudor-style apartment houses. Our bustling street was lined with four-story apartment buildings, each exquisitely unique, featuring vertical streamlines and curved corner balconies angled in romantic retro-futuristic juxtaposition.

Our landlord grew up in our apartment. He claimed that Jubilee Court was the most famous apartment complex in all of Shanghai. It had a wood-paneled, five-sided living room with large double-glazed windows on three walls, and an enormous master bedroom that was bigger than the entirety of most of the New York apartments I'd lived in. With built in closets, a soaking tub and a balcony that overlooked Fuxing Lu, I told Norman I wanted it before I even saw the second bedroom, or the dine-in kitchen with staff quarters, washer, drier and a guest bath.

As lovely as it was, there were some strange things about it too. For instance, all the countertops in the kitchen were intended for shorter people, about six inches lower than American countertops. There was no oven - only commercial bakeries have ovens. There's a strange dish-sterilizing cabinet, instead of a dishwasher, which I still don't understand. Through our interpreting realtor, the landlord told us to keep the guest-bath door closed and run water in there often, explaining that Shanghai has such shallow soil that the waste sometimes comes up through the drains. What a feature. We also had to get used to the constant droning megaphones outside of the dead-electronics collectors passing on bicycles, and the incessant ringing bells of recycling collectors working at all hours of the day and night.

At times I felt like I was an alien visiting another planet.

Gage brought his friend, Dougie Brookes, along for the ride. A pale Aussie, he greeted me enthusiastically with a wide, toothy grin, pink-flushed cheeks, and a firm handshake. He was considerably big compared to the rest of us, built like a football player at six-foot-three, but soft around the edges. With puppy dog eyes, he sported gelled back hair, pungent cologne, and pink, plaid Bermuda shorts and complimentary pastel t-shirt.

Gage was speaking Mandarin to our gatekeeper, an older woman who might have been quite attractive if she ever smiled instead of grimaced. She spent her days in a red Party armband sat in a three by three un-air-conditioned cell, drinking from a murky green cesspool of dodgy-looking tea in between naps on the small bare desk.

"Xie Xie, zài jiàn," Gage said to her, meaning 'thank you and good-bye'.

He said she was asking all kinds of questions about us, like where we're from, our ages, whether or not we were married, adding that we should get married, what our jobs were... Gage warned us that her real job is being the neighborhood busybody, knowing everyone's business and snitching to The Party.

"So whatever you do, don't get on her bad side. The Chinese character used for her job is the same one they use for spy," he added, leaving little doubt as to her true occupation.

We set out on our bicycling adventure towards Urumqi Lu. Families went zooming by us, five to a motorbike. Children stand in the front between a man's feet, while women sit sidesaddle on the back, some holding babies nonchalantly in one arm, loosely holding on with the other. At a red light, scores and scores of bikes lined up. I spotted a whole, recently slaughtered pig laid across the back of a motorbike. One bicycle, peddled by a small, tobacco-colored man puffing away on a cigarette that never touched his hands, was stacked with white Styrofoam boxes so thick in every direction it was the size of a small house. No joke.

A street shaded with trees, Urumqi Lu was lined with small shops selling single items. Open-front fruit stalls vividly colored the populous street. Storekeepers hung out on the sidewalks conversing with customers and neighbors, sometimes bickering loudly with their competition across the way. Older people sat on stools keeping an eye on the children playing in the running water taps on the sidewalk. Over the shops were shabby, barn-red apartments with skinny balconies that dipped in the center from old age. A man with a portable store on a wagon hitched to a bicycle sold furry toilet seat covers, hair-dye with a picture of Nicole Kidman on the box, socks with a picture of Jennifer Aniston on the label, and a bunch of kitchen and bathroom products. Oh yeah. And live, caged chickens too.

A guy in front of us stopped mid-stride, pressed his index finger against one nostril and exhaled hard. A stream of snot splattered onto the sidewalk. Then he did the other nostril, hawked up a loogie and continued on his way. Dougie and I looked at each other completely grossed out. I turned around to find Norman going into what I call 'Full-Tourette's', when he launches into full-on performance mode, regardless of location or who's looking. The sidewalk became his personal stage.

With arms stretched out wide, mouth towards the sky and eyes closed for dramatic effect, he sang at the top of his lungs, "Val- Lencia! Stick your head between your knees and whistle up your Barcelo-na! Sing along if you know the words!"

Sticking his bum out, he marched back and forth, throwing his fists in the air while singing the Robin Hood theme song with appropriate bow and arrow gestures. Sure enough, people began to gather. He encouraged them to applaud.

"Thank you, thank you very much!" he said waving to his new fans and wiggling his hips like Elvis. The crowd smiled, not knowing what to make of him. They don't make people like Norman in China.

If he loved one thing about Shanghai, it was that by doing almost anything, he could attract a big crowd of incredulous, gawking locals. The lower working-class were always up for a good laugh, especially when it came at the expense of weird foreigners. He was used to Manhattan where a thirty minute experiment once proved that if he stood on the corner of 8th Avenue and 34th Street outside Macy's, he could shout anything - obscenities, crazy talk, political manifestos, episodes of Sponge Bob Squarepants, anything - and no one would give a second look. Business as usual. All the world might be his stage, but in China he always played to a full house.

Not yet having enough, he took a woman's hand and got down on one knee to serenade her with another Norman original sung to 'Apple of my Eye'.

"You are the Ayi of my eye... I hope I never have to clean, with-out you!"

After a kiss on the hand and the desired response from the local swooning cougars, he was back up, on his bike and doing wheelies down the street. I'm used to these kinds of shenanigans, but it never fails to make me laugh, even if it's out of sheer embarrassment. Dougie and Gage on the other hand, were practically pissing themselves with laughter. Tears, turning red, all of it.

Live Poultry Street was next. It's just like a very crowded petting zoo full of animals and reptiles... that you can eat. Walking my bike, I saw a butcher decapitate a fish, proudly holding it up for his potential customers to see as it's lips continued to twitch and it's eyeballs shifted back and forth for almost a minute until the life finally left it. I felt a tug on my sleeve and looked down to see the sweet face of a little girl with a camera. I posed with her for a photograph, giving the mandatory peace sign. She liked my hair. A chicken making it's escape appeared at my feet, followed by a crouching, cursing woman who picked it up by the wings. Live turkeys lingered awaiting execution. Other vendors cover their portion of sidewalk with bins of blue water containing everything from crayfish and eels, to giant bullfrogs, and the delicacy called gooey duck, which looks like a giant penis and ballsack. None for me thanks.

We continued east, stopping at a yellow Buddhist temple surrounded by stores selling incense and pink lotus candles. In the windows were funny, weightless, paper versions of things like sneakers, cellphones, cars, doll-size townhouses, fruit, stacks of fake money, Rolexes, and Louis Vuitton suits and sunglasses. Gage says that these things get burned for the dead who are believed to receive the gifts in heaven or where ever, to literally use in their afterlife. The concept of needing a Rolex to tell time, or a flash Burberry handbag in an afterlife was quite a concept for me to wrap my head around, but the bold consumerist eccentricity of it interests me.

"This stuff is Confucian, but most Chinese are godless. Or they'll be a little Confucian, a little Taoist, and a little Buddhist to cover all their bases just in case," said Gage. "American Christians are starting to move in on them now, to capitalize on the godless, new-money, middle-class, selling them Bibles and the legends of Jesus."

Gage announced that we were about to enter *real* China. Crossing the street onto Fengbang Lu, I was in a swarm of buzzing pedestrians, motorbikes, and the random unfortunate car caught between the clothing rails, blowing the horn. A group of teenage boys wearing baggy jeans, sneakers and hip-hop inspired t-shirts stood outside a hair salon smoking cigarettes, each in slightly different versions of the same uneven, spiky haircut. The hair-boys who work at the salons were by far the coolest looking local guys. Refreshingly style conscious and always surrounded by a gaggle of giggly girls. Blankets laid in the road selling waving Mao watches, ceramic statues of proud peasants straddling rockets, jade jewelry, cigarette girl repro-posters, Saddam Hussein playing cards, and a heap of Che Guevara merchandise. A barber was shaving a man in his outdoor barbershop of a reclining chair and mirror, with a makeshift shoeshine facility next to it.

I passed a woman holding a crying toddler with his little wrinkled butt hanging out of a purpose-made hole in his pants. This makes it easy for the baby to pee and poo on the street or sidewalk whenever nature calls. The Chinese don't believe in diapers after the first twelve months. Next to the mother, a suitcase full of hot pink four-inch rubber dildos, whirling and circling mindlessly, which poses the question: *Only four inches?*

Suddenly, there was a cacophony of horns, bells and shouting. The woman selling the cocks sprang up abruptly, throwing her red-faced toddler under arm, scrambling to zip up her suitcase as fast as she could with the other. She shrieked. In seconds, all the merchants and floggers were swooping to pick up their blankets. Uniformed police officers were filing out of vans to bust them. They started to rough guys up, kicking over tables. I bent down to help the mother stuff things into her case. Then I heard my name being called from the distance. Like snapping out of a daydream, I realized that I needed to get out of there too, and fast.

Across the intersection were the remains of a neighborhood the size of a city block, reduced to dirt and rubble, leveled by bulldozers. It was evident that people still lived in what remained of the run down shacks missing walls and roofs. Old people sat outside as if guarding the only home they'd ever known. Scavenged items lay strewn amongst the dirt, once loved stuffed animals, framed photos of smiling children and grandparents. Kids were trying to sell these found items on their own tiny blankets by the side of the road. A young boy ran up a castle made of debris, pointed his arm in the air, counted to five and then ran after the other children, wonderfully oblivious to the wreckage of their environment.

"The government owns all the property in China," Gage told us. "If they want to build a new road or business center, even if it means destroying whole communities and displacing thousands of people, they just do it. It's happening everywhere in China, creating controversy like never before. They aren't offering proper compensation to people either, leaving those forced from their homes without enough money to move anywhere else. You won't read about this stuff in the papers though. They don't want anyone to know. And the people who protest? Who knows... They disappear."

The most extraordinary woman I'd ever seen came out of a disheveled hut. Mid-fifties, her skin was dyed the color of a coconut. She stood in a doorway shouting shrilly at her husband and hunch-backed son who were repairing a motorbike on the street. A mango-colored beehive sat on top of her head reaching up a good ten inches, like Marge Simpson's Chinese twin sister. She had little figurines of a squirrel and a bird perched in the honeycomb of hair, peeking out the wide, hair-sprayed curls. She wore a bright orange, pink and yellow floral print muumuu and round, rose-tinted glasses. She looked like something out of a cartoon.

Gage pointed to the bamboo ready to be assembled into scaffolding.

"All these perfectly great streets are getting replaced with stupid boutiques. Like the night market by People's Square. You have to go to it now because it won't exist in a few weeks. It's so frustrating because this is the stuff foreigners and tourists love about China, but the Chinese don't get that. This whole city is getting a facelift because they're starting to get ready for the World Expo in 2010. Beijing's getting one right now for the Olympics, but it's our turn next. I for one am not looking forward to it."

He told me that the World Expo is like a World's Fair. They were predicting between fifty and seventy million people in town for it over a six-month period.

"That'll be great for your business," Dougie pointed out, lighting up a cigarette.

"It really jumps out at me," Norman interjected, "That they've gone from being simple peasants essentially, to all this, overnight. Like a snap of a finger. You can see the older people are in shock. They lived through the Cultural Revolution remember. Countries like China and Japan never went through their own Age of Enlightenment. They've received all the benefits from ours, which cost us millions of lives and two hundred years, out of which came the platform for all modern science, art, philosophy, and the Industrial Revolution. But China never went through the process to get to this point. The trial and error. I can't see how this deficiency won't come back to haunt them, probably sooner rather than later."

On the way home we stopped for massages. Two hours, a hundred kwai. That's about fourteen USD. So cool. After exchanging business cards with both hands and a bow as custom predicates, Dougie and Norman arranged to meet later in the week. Dougie had a background in the food and beverage industry, and he was interested to learn more about the club project. Then I kissed the boys on each cheek goodbye.

The wind picked up as the sun went down. We passed older couples waltzing on a patch of sidewalk to a symphony, charmingly distorted from a crackling cassette player. We went by families having dinner outside on the lanes, drinking Tsingtao píjiǔ, and kindly inviting us to join them. Multiple generations sat on lawn chairs in the middle of a low traffic street. Everyone in pajamas or boxer shorts like a giant slumber party, watching a singing dwarf play a ukulele on a communal television set.

I peddled, the night air hitting my face. In that moment I knew.

I'd been at a crossroads in my life. As an actress it was either move to LA, wait tables, and hope someone discovered me, or move to Shanghai, open a nightclub, be with my lover and create my own destiny. I knew I'd made the right decision.

The perpetual forward motion of life moved under me like a treadmill and I flashed on a photograph in time. I was in high school, sat on top of a hill in Centreville, Virginia, tripping on mushrooms with my best friend, as you do, listening to the cars on Route 66. At the exact same second, we both had a massive epiphany. Convinced we'd discovered the meaning of life, we wrote it down on a pack of Camel lights in case we forgot it the next morning.

It said:

We have to keep moving forward.

The memory spread a smile over my lips. Yes we do. Words to live by.

I stood at the kitchen sink washing dishes, wondering why we decided to only have Ayi come once a week instead of everyday like most expats. I admired the framed cut-and-paste job Norman did on an old propaganda poster. He replaced the giant head of Chairman Mao looking down over cheering peasants, with a blown up image of his own mugging face. Calling himself 'Arm-Chairman Gosney', and titling it, 'My Plan for China'.

"I've got it," Norman said, charging into the kitchen.

"Yeah?" He had to wait until I got the muck out from under my fingernails before I could care about whatever it was that he got.

"Seriously, I think I've got it, the name for the club. Only if you like it, of course. You ready? Okay. I think we should call the place... Chinatown."

It produced an instant grin on my face. "Gosney & Kallman's CHINATOWN! What do you think? Do you like it?"

Hearing my second name next his caught me off guard.

"Well, I'd like to think we're in this thing together," he said. I dried my hands and threw my arms around his neck, squeezing tightly. My eyes welled up. I was incredibly touched.

"I love it," I said when I could find my words again.

"It makes reference to everything. It says it all."

We sat down at the kitchen table, our mutual excitement boiling over. Norman sketched what would become our logo, an old black and white, illuminated sign, just like the old Chinese ones. *Gosney & Kallman's* in small letters arched across the top, with CHINATOWN in block letters going straight down, and *Shanghai* across the bottom.

"Every major city has a Chinatown and now Shanghai will have one too. In most cities, you see, it's where East meets West, but here it's where West meets East. Also, it's a great film, I mean, come on, Jack Nicholson!"

"Opening a Chinatown in China...?" I mused whimsically, before laughing out loud. "I think it's absolutely hilarious. Let's do it!"

I couldn't believe I was about to own the first burlesque nightclub in Asia.

CHAPTER 6 – Trip to Chinatown

Norman made me Director of Show. He figured that with my theatrical background and organizational skills that I could handle preparing the show at the heart of the Chinatown experience, while he worried about setting up the business and building the premises.

"Are you sure?" I asked. "You really think I can be a director?"

"You can be anything you want to be. This is China."

Being Director of Show was a huge responsibility. I was to come up with, develop and execute all the material, dances, production numbers, and be the overall manager of the cast and crew. I'd never been completely in charge of the show before, but I was ready to give it my everything. I desperately wanted to get it right too, to prove to everyone, myself most of all, that I deserved to be there, that my talents were worthy of an opportunity like this, that I wasn't just there because I was Norman's girlfriend, and to show everyone that our shows really are the best in the world.

When Norman first introduced me to the world of burlesque, I found it quite intimidating. All the women were beautiful, confident, empowered, and now I can say it: Fiercely territorial. Showgirls like Shelly Bomb, Lady Ace, Ms.Tickle, Angie Pontani, Julie Atlas Muz, Ami Goodheart, and Dirty Martini were the trailblazers in the rebirth of this art form in the mid-'90's in New York. Along with producers like Norman and Tony Marando, this group of innovators created an industry and a market where there simply hadn't been one before.

Some people like to trace the origins of burlesque back as far as the ancient Greeks, but the word *burlesque* derives from the Italian *burlesco* or *burla*, meaning satire or mockery, often referring to an act or literary work intended to cause laughter by caricaturing the manner or spirit of serious works.

Burlesque first came into fashion during the Victorian era in London, taking the form of musical theatre parody and political pantomime. The birth of burlesque as we know it today is thanks to two main sources: The English rose, Lydia Thompson and her British Blondes, who set New York into a frenzy when they arrived in 1868; And 19th century Paris, the age of The Can Can, the *Folies Bergère* and the Moulin Rouge. With hard work, training and talent, a girl could transcend her background and class through performance, enticing the hearts and imaginations of kings, nobility, artists and writers.

During the 20th century burlesque became a main attraction on the stages of New York City. Inspired by *Folies Bergère*, Flo Ziegfeld brought the showgirl chorus line to Broadway with *The Ziegfeld Follies* in 1907, producing extravaganzas and high-class vaudeville variety shows featuring the likes of Josephine Baker, Fanny Brice, Louise Brooks, Bob Hope, Will Rogers, and W.C. Fields, et al. From this world, when it was the premiere form of entertainment, came the legend of what it means to be a showgirl. Showgirls represent a model of femininity, beauty, mystery, glamour, and power. They were well-regarded professionals, notorious society girls, and emulated celebrities.

During the 1930's burlesque became more associated with female nudity, or the act of striptease, with vaudeville theatres, such as Billy Minsky's Winter Garden, featuring comedians like Red Skelton and Abbot and Costello on the same bill as Lili St. Cyr, Ann Corio, and the most famous burlesque artist of all time, Miss Gypsy Rose Lee. Films of the 1940's and 50's glamourized the image of the showgirl with the likes of Jane Mansfield and Marilyn Monroe leading the way. By the 1960's though, a new era was ushered in and burlesque became 'Burlesk', synonymous with strip clubs and grindhouse.

Burlesque as art went into hiding for several decades, but in the mid-90's it offered the perfect alternative to the popular rave and electronica scene for those seeking something new and naughty, the next big thing. Norman was at the forefront of the movement, opening a genuine speakeasy on 23rd Street, Dutch

Weismann's, a clandestine cabaret experiment that changed burlesque and variety in America. He went on to design and open the original Slipper Room, regarded as the ground zero of burlesque, a permanent X on the map of Manhattan nightlife. Then he designed and operated SHOW nightclub in Times Square where he had a ten-girl chorus line, before trading it in for the more intimate venue of our speakeasy, The Blushing Diamond.

As you can see, there was a lot to live up to. I didn't just want to re-produce the same shows we did in New York either, I wanted to build a Shanghai burlesque and new-vaudeville identity that paid tribute to all those legendary showgirls who came before and their daring, imaginative, lust-for-life spirit.

That being said, producing our kinds of shows in China was completely new territory. The challenges I faced were monumental and would probably be enough to put a lot of people off, but I always try to see challenges as unique opportunities for creative possibilities. Here are some of the things I needed to consider:

1.   **Language** - I couldn't rely on either spoken English or Chinese. The acts had to speak a universal language, one that I got to make up essentially, using slapstick, gimmicks, scintillating exchanges, pantomime, sets, props, characterization and costumes. I could no longer perform my trademark, spoken word pieces where I pick a movie out of a hat and perform 'Any Movie in 3-Minutes', as it would risk alienating and losing half our audience. Determined to use this language barrier as an advantage, I would have occasions in the shows when only Chinese speakers

could get a certain joke, and visa versa.

2.   **Reference** – I had to anticipate that the majority of customers wouldn't have seen anything comparable to the kind of theatre we do before. Unlike straight theatre where there is a church-like division between performer and audience, our shows are truly interactive. We have to fight for attention over drinking and sex-play. It's ballsy, hardcore and difficult, but when we get it right, it's one of the best nights of your life. But there's nothing remotely like this kind of entertainment in the Chinese culture. To explain what we do to the Chinese we ended up describing it as, 'A Broadway show in a 1930's theme bar'. But it wasn't just the Chinese. Shanghai's a truly international city, and I wanted to impress those who had also been to the Moulin Rouge, or witnessed burlesque coming up in cities around the UK, AU, and US.

A further consideration was the new generation, who were used to having their entertainment mediated through a monitor, some having never seen live performance before. There was no relying on cultural reference points that brought easy laughs and were easy to take for granted. Therefore, I had the once in a lifetime opportunity to introduce, train, and educate my audiences from scratch. No pressure or anything...

3.   **Burlesque** - Technically speaking, burlesque or any kind of under-clothed public display, is illegal in China. But anything is possible, and under further investigation I found that the qualm was with nudity, not the *act* of stripping per se. I took this clarification as good news. I'd still have to be extremely careful with the handling of this controversial element, as getting it

wrong could land me in jail... So there was that.

4.   **Chinese** - I wanted to incorporate Chinese inspired acts into every show. Acting as a formal bow to our host country, it would give the Chinese face and hopefully garner their support, without which we would have little chance of succeeding. The challenge was my lack of reference to what would turn the Chinese on stage-wise, so I'd have to work on that.

I started researching Shanghai in the 1920's and '30's. At my local DVD store I was surprised to find not just modern blockbusters, but also a huge back catalogue of classics and obscurities, including the quintessential films of Hollywood's dramatic take on the exotic, mysterious city of Shanghai. Movies that played to the West's romanticized love affair with The Paris of the Orient. I watched such Vaseline lensed classics as *Shanghai Express* (1932), *The Shanghai Gesture* (1941), and *The Lady from Shanghai* (1947). I saw Marlene Dietrich as a perfect fantasy customer, vamping at the bar, downing cocktails, hustling both the boys and girls. The bootleg DVD industry is rumored to be run by the army, blatantly ignoring international copyright laws. I'm not complaining because DVDs were sold for the equivalent of one USD, one of my favorite things about life in Shanghai.

There was a nightclub from the 1940's that I latched onto in Chinatown, San Francisco, called The Forbidden City. Headed by the impresario Charlie Low, it inspired the nightclub featured in the 1961 musical *Flower Drum Song*. The Forbidden City's bills advertised The Chinese Frank Sinatra, The Chinese

Fred Astaire and Ginger Rogers, and The Chinese Carmen Miranda. Charlie Low discovered the two most famous oriental showgirls: Miss Noel Toy, known as The Chinese Sally Rand, specializing in a white ostrich feather fan dance; and Miss Joy Ching, Toy's eventual replacement in 1941, who was famous for her act 'The Girl in the Gilded Cage'. Dancers Dorothy Sun and Mary Mammon became later attractions as well. After the nightclub's success, competition followed. The Chinatown Sky Room boasted a strictly Chinese line up including six dancing showgirls called The Wongettes; the Kubla Khan club featuring the Kubla Dancers, and Fong Wan's Club Oakland starring the famous exotic dancer Barbara Yung, all sprang up shortly after. Discovering the history of Chinese-American nightclub entertainment filled me with a sense of duty and pride about my position in upholding the dynasty of tradition with a twist.

In all my extensive research, I uncovered little that threw light on the cabaret and jazz scene fabled to exist in Shanghai. I think that most likely the myths are truths, but the evidence of the rumored gregarious times of opium, prostitution, jazz, taxi dancing, gallivanting and debauchery must have been tragically destroyed during the Revolution, along with everything else. For the authorities, that whole period in history has essentially been erased, though lǎowài enthusiasts are starting to dig deeper, and uncover the odd jewel.

I started to keep a blog, Diary of a Shanghai Showgirl, that followed my research and experiences in China so my friends and family back home could get a sense of the love affair I was having with this city.

Because blogs and other social media, like Facebook and Twitter, are blocked in China, I used a proxy, and while I was always conscious to be careful what I wrote, I figured that because these sites were already blocked that it was out of the Chinese domain and I could take a few liberties with inferences here and there, making my true opinions known by speaking between the lines.

One day, out of the blue, warning messages in Chinese started popping up in a continuant stream on my computer, until it couldn't take it anymore and shut itself down. I started to freak out. Was my computer was being hacked? I tried to remember if I had any emails or posted anything that could've brought this on. I knew better than to ever mention The Three T's: Tibet, Tiananmen or Taiwan. Then I remembered a photo I posted of a beautiful Chinese woman smoking a pipe, and realized the caption on the photo made reference to the Opium Wars.

My computer crashed. I ended up having to reload the original software to make it work again. I was blocked from my email and blog, even when I tried to log on with Norman's computer. Several friends confirmed that it was no coincidence. I'd red-flagged myself to the government by daring to post something with the words 'Opium Wars' and now my online activity was being monitored and investigated by the authorities. It took five days before I was able to get back into my hotmail account. There I found seventy-two emails I'd never seen before marked as read. Big Brother was watching me, and he had definitely made his presence known.

Norman rode his bike up and down every street in Shanghai for weeks on end until, after many false starts, he found the building for Chinatown. It was on Zhapu Lu, a very old, very famous Shanghainese restaurant street, completely unlike anything else in the city. It looked like what I'd imagined Shanghai would look like before arriving and seeing just how modern it is. The narrow street was lined in neon signs like the original Vegas strip. It reminded me of a Chinese version of Bourbon Street in New Orleans. The street had a timeless quality, or a quality of being trapped in time, with sharks swimming in tanks in the windows of dodgy-looking seafood restaurants. Prostitutes dressed like full-on hookers pulling Johns outside of pink-lit storefronts. Competitive barkers trying to get you into their joints. Rough-looking locals in bathrobes, drinking from bottles in the afternoon on their balconies, shouting down at the people on automated rickshaws passing below. It felt dangerous and filthy, but in a sexy way that was exciting and turned me on. And our fantasy building, the future home of Chinatown, was just at the end of it, over Haining Lu.

An abandoned Buddhist Temple. My heart skipped a beat as I stood admiring the property. The top half of the building's front was in the shape of a conch shell, like The Birth of Venus. The bottom half boasted a sculptured frieze with anthropomorphic animals and Buddhist demigods displayed over twenty different mandalas. The entire façade was rendered in glowing, honey-colored sandstone. It was a completely unique, one-off masterpiece. The wackiest most beautiful building in a city full of wacky and beautiful buildings.

The plaque outside read:

> Heritage Protected Buddhist Temple, built in 1931 by a Japanese architect as a Nishi Honganji, which is a Japanese 'friendly society' meeting hall. Designed in the style of Hindu architecture with allusions to the Chaitya Hall that stands in the former Japanese/Jewish section of town.

So, to summarize: A Japanese designer, in Hindu style architecture, in the Jewish concession, in Shanghai, in the 1930's...? I mean, Wow! Could it get any cooler? It already looked like a cabaret club from a black and white Hollywood film. I could imagine gangster's molls draped in sequins and furs, strolling through the doors on the arms of cigar-smoking high-rollers, out for a night of saucy entertainment. It was perfect.

"I haven't been this excited about a building since we found the church on 6th Avenue and turned it into Limelight," Norm recalled.

He's owned, designed, or operated some of the world's most definitive nightclubs over the years, including Danceteria, Limelight, Nell's, P1 in Munich, Gold in Tokyo, and over a hundred more.

"Those were the good old days."

"No," I corrected him. "*These* are the good old days."

We decided to break in. We squeezed through the small space between the chained doors into a domed entryway to have a snoop around our future premises - something we refer to in America as 'breaking and entering'. The building was derelict.

Most recently it had been a KTV, and before that, a snooker parlor, but it had been vacant for the last seven years and was rapidly dilapidating.

A dank smell wafted over us as we crawled inside. Shining our flashlights around, I could see it was bigger than I expected. The entrance had pink and black marble floors and there was a busted, dried-up fountain adorned in a string of fake ivy. That would have to go. To the left, a grand staircase twisting up to the second floor. I walked forward into the darkness shining my torch. Under the stairs, a bar. At the same time we both flashed our lights on a dug out enclave in the center of the eastern wall: A natural place for a stage!

Norman estimated it was about 8,000 square feet, including the second floor. He began designing it out loud. He'd keep the doors, staircase and bar, refurbishing them of course.

"It's a great size; not too huge, not too small. I can seat about two hundred, two-fifty in here comfortably. I'll line the wall across the back with banquets, make cozy, plush sections on tiers of raked seating. We'll have cane-back chairs and tables all around the front of the stage, you know, like The Copacabana in *Goodfellas*. And later in the night it can become the dance floor. I can see the stage right there. Plunk. Can't you? Maybe a bandstand to the right. I could put in a streetlamp that lights up, you know I love to do things like that. And then, to the left there, the emcee's pulpit, or cage. Give him something to shout from."

"What about a Juliet balcony just above it in the heavens? We could feature a singer up there. Use it to misdirect attention between acts?" I suggested.

"Yes. Yes, I believe we can. Good idea."

The only remaining relics from the building's past were leftovers from the KTV, which apparently had an Egyptian theme. Humungous statues of pharaohs, free-standing, bare-breasted slave women balancing bowls on their heads, a concrete mock pyramid twenty-feet in the air with the face of King Tut at the apex, and last, but certainly not least, sculptures of crouched black slaves holding up tables on their necks and backs.

When we finished poking around we crawled back out of the building into the daylight. Invigorated by the potential gem we had on hand, we stood in the middle of the street staring in awe.

"My only concern," I said, playing devil's advocate, "Is that it's a bit off the beaten track. But otherwise, I love it."

"I thought that at first too, but really it's not. You just don't recognize where we are. See, the Bund is right there, in spitting distance. The new Hyatt is opening around the corner. The 1933 project's one block away. This is the coming area, you can already see it happening."

Norman has a knack for having a finger on the Zeitgeist.

"You know, I've always said this: Being a destination is not a bad thing at all. Like when we opened Area in Tribeca, or Mars in the Meatpacking district. We were the first people to do anything in those areas and that acts as a draw. An advantage. People are always looking for something new. The next big thing. And you know, I really think a lot of tourists come here looking for that vision of Shanghai in the

'20's and '30's, and I can't believe no one's catering to that experience. What I like about this location is that it isn't a tourist spot yet. It's authentic. It's real. And it feels like a secret. A buried treasure waiting to be discovered. That's one of the ways we'll sell this baby."

I was sold.

Now we just had to figure out how to convince the owners to let us turn it into the hottest nightclub in the world. And, of course, when I say owners, I mean the Chinese government.

CHAPTER 7 – Naked Next to a Showgirl

I stripped off my sweaty gym clothes and wrapped a towel around my naked body in one swift move. We joined The Ambassy Club, opposite the American consulate complex on Hengshan Lu. Holding the towel tight to my chest, I flip-flopped to the steam room. Local women don't worry about such modesty. The older ones often hang around with nothing on, chatting loudly for hours, their concave bottoms suctioned to the plastic stools. I admired their oblivious, nonchalant attitude, but I did find it a bit much when they lifted one leg up onto the counter and took a blow drier to their sprawling forest of black bushy pubic hair, never missing a beat in conversation. In general, waxing, shaving and trimming didn't appear to be much of a concern. Meanwhile, Norman was getting a big kick out of strutting around the guy's locker room towel-free, unapologetically putting his substantial manhood on display, showing off the proof that he was indeed a bigger man than the rest of them.

In the sauna, I laid down on my towel breathing the hard oak vapors deep into my lungs. Eyes closed, beads of sweat sliding down my skin. To me, this was the best part about working out. I'd been making a point to embrace a healthy lifestyle, smug with myself for having kicked the tobacco habit, but my lungs were still under constant pressure from the dense haze of pollution.

After a few minutes, the sauna door opened, jarring my attention. It was the girl I spied earlier dancing alone in one of the yoga studios. She stood in silhouette in the doorway like a China doll, steam rising up around her naked body as she made her entrance. For a long moment I couldn't take my eyes off her. Svelte body, pierced belly button, boyish dark nipples and long, bow legs. Very attractive. About my age I guessed, with short, black bobbed hair framing her round, high-cheek-boned face. She caught me staring and smiled at me directly. I remembered what Gage said about foreign women feeling insecure next to local girls and now I understood why. She made herself comfortable, lying down on the wooden tier above mine.

After a few minutes her voice cut through the thick, salty air in short stabs of high-pitched sound.

"Where-you-from?"

My eyes opened, startled to see her face looking down at mine, our mouths within inches. Her eyes, purple.

"Um... New York... America." She'd caught me off guard.

"Wow. U-S-A. I love U-S-A." She spoke every word in syllables, in a way I found oddly adorable.

"Have you ever been to the USA?"

"No, but very much I want that." She put her head back down, releasing her intimate gaze to my relief.

"I saw you dancing just now. You're really good. Are you a dancer?"

"Yes, I am dancer. I love dance. My parents don't like, she want me to be married, have baby, but I don't want."

Her voice got very high on that last declaration. She was funny. I got the feeling that I was going to like this girl.

She continued, "I am young. Why do I want to mar-rieee?"

Marriage was a big deal here, much more so than in the States. If a girl isn't married by the time she's twenty-seven, she's written off as an old maid, an Ayi. On the weekends in People's Square, parents of young bachelors and bachelorettes gather to match-make in the park. They bring photos of their kid, as well as copies of their grades and proof of apartment ownership, in order to find a worthy partner for their child to marry.

"Where do you dance?"

"I am a teach. And I do sexy dance."

"Teacher?"

"Yes, teacher, my English so bad, you are very beau-ti-ful," she said, as if it was all one thought.

"Thank you." I never know how to take that particular compliment. "You're very beautiful too." In fact, she was the most beautiful Chinese girl I'd ever seen.

"So, I'm opening up a nightclub here," I continued, "But different from others. More like a theatre, stage, you know?" I was speaking in a newly adopted, simplistic manner, with a hint of a local accent.

"We do shows, like Broadway? Um... singing, sexy dance, showgirls?"

She sat up on her elbows and looked at me, and I tried not to stare at her tiny brown nipples.

"Yes, I want to be. I am very good, you'll like it."

And with that, she laid her head back down and I closed my eyes once again. I could sympathize with all those guys out there with yellow-fever, as they call it. I was getting a wave of yellow-fever myself. For a second, I imagined this scenario like the start of a porno. Rubbing hands across stomachs, lightly kissing lips and breasts, hands between legs... Rubbing away the sweat that was rolling down my stomach, I flashed on the last time I found myself naked next to a showgirl.

A lot of the showgirls at The Blushing Diamond were into other girls. Or had been at one point. It was like some unwritten showgirl initiation or something, being gay or being bi-curious, at least. Sometimes after work the showgirls would end up back at someone's apartment. The booze would flow. Clothes naturally came off. Someone might offer a massage or we might play truth or dare.... Girls would start to get frisky and play with each other. Kissing, licking, rubbing, while others watched or joined in. Sometimes it would be innocent, all fun and games, but other times it was like a spell came over everyone, like a sexual trance.

Shortly before leaving New York one of the lesbians decided that she had fallen in love with me and persuaded me to see what it was like to be with a woman. It took me a few weeks before I realized that she was crazy and the relationship was a huge mistake.

She turned abusive and possessive, and I came running back to Norman. Begged him to take me back. I promised never to stray again, for a man or a woman, and if anything, it confirmed how much I really loved him, and how much I really wanted to make our relationship work, despite our considerable age gap. But I knew I needed more than a second chance. We needed a new beginning. This was the unspoken secret behind my eagerness to move to the other side of the world.

"What is your name?"

Her voice startled me, bringing me out of the past and back into the sweaty present. A shiver shot down my spine.

"My name? Amelia. We'll have to exchange cards. I'm going to go and shower now, I'm getting too hot."

That was an understatement.

"But I'll see you in the locker room, okay? What's your name?"

"Star," she replied. Great name. It fit her.

One of the many unique names I'd heard since being there. In school, the students are required to study English and pick their own Western name. Some go for a name that sounds similar to their Chinese one, like Lynn for Ling. Others use it as a rare opportunity for self-expression. That's when you get the good ones. The first time I met my friend Dream she told me with a straight face, 'My boyfriend calls me Nightmare'. I ran across a Smell, an Afraid, a Little Punk, and even a Urine, though I really hope that's not the way he spells it. Personal favorites of mine are Icy Ho and Rainbow Goo.

The one that takes the cake though was the ever-popular urban legend that people swear is true, though I can't say I ever met the girl personally. Supposedly, there was this very cute, innocent Chinese girl who was pursued by a lǎowài guy. After she finally went to bed with him, she asked him to give her a beautiful English name. So he did. He gave her Chlamydia.

CHAPTER 8 – Thirteen O'clock

Crawling into the backseat of a taxi, I spit out the words "Xiè xiè nǐ. Nǐ hǎo. Wǒmen chū Yue Yuan, hǎo de?" or 'Thank you (for stopping for a foreigner and not being a dick and driving past me like the rest of them), Hello, We go to Yue Gardens, Okay?'

My Mandarin was making progress, but it still took three times before the driver smugly said, "Ah, Yue Yuan!" which, I swear, was the exact same way I had just said it.

I was finding the language really difficult. It uses tongue positions that feel unnatural and it was hard for me to differentiate between some of the sounds, but I knew I needed to make the effort if I ever wanted to be accepted in this country, since it looked like we were going to be there for awhile. It's not a pretty language by any means. It often sounds guttural and mean to my ears, making regular conversations sound like disgruntled shouting matches.

My Chinese tutor, Winnie, came twice a week. Very childish and straight-laced for someone in her late twenties. Having grown up in the American public school system, the first thing I wanted to know was how to say bad words, of course. This caused quite a sensation for Winnie. A hand in front of her face, giggles, books in front of her face, embarrassed squirms. It was far more of a reaction than I had anticipated. Eventually, I got a few naughty words out of her. My favorite expression was a Shanghainese insult, 'Nǐ shí sān diǎn', or 'You're thirteen o'clock', which is considered a nasty insult that means someone is really stupid. Many of the other swear words generally translate to 'Crawl back into your mother'.

Approaching Yue Gardens, a famously inexpensive area of souvenir shops, notion stalls and two-kwai stores, I could see the tops of traditional Chinese buildings. Sloping canopy roofs in red tile that peak at the corners, and tall pagodas like timber wedding cakes. My mission was to source materials and prices for making the showgirl costumes, something I love to do.

Most burlesque artists appreciate the complete control they have over their personal performances, developing everything themselves, from concept and choosing and editing music, to making their own costumes and props. My favorite burlesque artists are famous for the imaginative stories they tell and their inventive reveals. While I couldn't wait to start on these individual production numbers, today my focus was pricing feathers, knickers, bras and rhinestones.

The taxi dropped me off in front of a McDonald's. Feeling a bit homesick and against my better judgment, I went inside and had a sneaky cheeseburger, coke and fries, savoring every sinful bite. With that wicked Western indulgence out of the way,

I began my exploration through the crowded sidewalks. The Chinese and foreign tourists pushed and shoved, taking pictures of themselves in front of hollow gold dragons in this bogus replica of an ancient village.

Hustlers followed me, touching my arms saying, "Watch? Bag? Watch? Bag?"

I shook my palm in their direction, making a point not to meet their eyes.

"Bù yào! Bù yào!" I said harshly in a tone that reflected theirs. Satisfied that I wasn't a tourist, they then left me alone.

I walked into a chaotic warehouse jam-packed with booths selling just about anything under the sun that could possibly be classified as 'Bits-and-Bobs' or 'Cheap Chinese Shit'. It was insane. Each little stall specialized in something different, from buttons and zippers, to underwear and wigs. And the prices, they must be the lowest in the world. The sequins appliqués I use to make my showgirl costumes that cost five dollars each in New York only cost five kwai here. Not even one dollar. I'd hit the jackpot!

Practicing my bargaining skills I used the phrase 'Tài guì le!' emphatically, meaning 'too expensive'. This never failed to get a jolted look of surprise, followed by a smile and a slight decrease in price. Never accept a first offer, it's guaranteed to be at least twice what they'd offer a local. And I walk away a few times, that always works too. Sometimes bargaining can get rather animated and a crowd will form of good-natured bystanders, usually rooting for me and my funny Virginian–New Yorker-Chinese. When it's all over, people pat me on the back and give a thumbs-up, congratulating me for giving the seller a hard time and haggling.

For ten kwai I bought Norman a swamp green sweater that features two knitted, naked, dreadlocked Rasta's with disproportionately giant, erect willies. Being both the ugliest and funniest sweater I'd ever seen, I bought it because I didn't think anyone would believe me when I tried to describe it. All over there were shirts with English words on them that didn't make any sense. A pretty teenage girl wore one that read 'Rear Load Here', and then an old granny had a shirt on that said 'Sex Machine'.

Then I found the shoe stalls. A pair of four-inch red vinyl stilettos, open toe with a strap, called my name. When I saw that they were only forty-nine kwai, the equivalent of seven USD, I knew it was meant to be. I asked for them in my size, a size 40, but I was horrified when the salesclerk told me that shoe sizes only go up to size 39. Anything over is for export only. Same with the clothes and the bras - everything was too small for me. I know it sounds cliché and terribly girlie, but honestly... The thought that I was living in a place where I couldn't buy shoes or bras or clothes was kind of devastating. I held back tears.

It wasn't just the shoes. Some days I could really feel the strain of living in a foreign culture. I felt like I couldn't connect, which is lonely. And shopping, something that usually cheers me up, was only making it worse. I decided I'd better call it a day.

Outside clouds formed overhead, threatening to break any minute as I hustled to get a cab. Droplets of rain started to splatter, as the hunt for a taxi became cutthroat. Being a ruthless New Yorker, I had a slight advantage and managed to get one pretty fast. I slid into the front seat next to the driver, feeling courageously Chinese as they often sit up front when riding solo in the cabs. I noticed this cab didn't have the regular plastic partition between the driver and passenger seats, but we had already taken off and the driver seemed to understand my Chinese and hadn't given me any trouble when I told him where I wanted to go.

To make the most of the journey, I pulled out my vocabulary flashcards and began to chat to the darkly tanned man with a mouth full of black teeth. He kept looking over at me and grinning, staring at me more than he was looking at the road. Sinking into the far corner of my seat, I began to regret sitting up front and speaking with him.

When the taxi pulled up in front of Jubilee Court, I put my hand out to pay him. He snatched the cash and grabbed my wrist, as his other hand came towards me. He squeezed both my breasts, first the right and then the left, like checking the firmness of fruit at the market. I was in shock. What the *fuck* was that? Without thinking, I smacked him hard in the face, then scrambled to get out of the car, falling ass first onto the wet pavement. The car sped off as I stood in the middle of the street shouting:

"Nǐ shí sān diǎn Mother-fucker! Nǐ shí sān diǎn!"

Our courtyard spy came out of her cave and asked me with gestures what the problem was. I described the incident in a silent pantomime: *Pointing to road, steering wheel. Hello! Sit down, talking, shock! Dick-boy's hands on my tits. More shock! Angry. Tā shí sān diǎn!* The woman nodded her head, but instead of being outraged like I was, she started to laugh. She made two big curves over her own flat chest, wiggling her hips making fun of me, pointing to the road, then making a sly-dog face. And then she came towards me, laughing away, pretending to honk my boobs. As if they hadn't been traumatized enough!

For weeks it had been cold, wet, windy, and miserable. All we wanted to do was hibernate and watch entire seasons of *The Wire* in one sitting. Everyone got sick with the repetitive Shanghai illness that comes and goes. The larger world was sick too. The global economic crisis had truly sunk its teeth in. While we expats scoffed at it, congratulating ourselves on having the foresight to be in the East as opposed to the West, it still affected us nonetheless.

All we really wanted to do was open the nightclub, but it was taking forever to wade through the red-tape, and just trying to get to the bottom of who actually owned our future premises was like going down a rabbit hole. In the meantime, we started taking side jobs as 'foreign faces' at press conferences and concerts that wanted to appear foreigner friendly. It proved to be quite easy, profitable work, and occasionally it was as interesting and hilarious as it was mind-numbingly boring. Norman got a modeling gig through Gage as a 'Mature lǎowài' in a high-profile ad campaign for China Telecom to run during the Olympics.

I got a reoccurring role in a Chinese soap opera playing a Russian nurse during World War II. The Chinese have deep-seeded hatred towards the Japanese, a result in part of the wartime Nanking massacre and in part because totalitarian regimes need constant enemies, scapegoats for their own shortcomings. Consequently, their entire entertainment industry is obsessed with the war and demonizing Japan, which was the basic premise of the television series I was in. Chinese actors play the Japanese characters though, a fact I find rather amusing. I learned my lines in English and later they were dubbed over in Chinese. The style of direction was very particular: 'Take three steps forward, put your hand to your heart, tilt your head this way this much and hold for three, take a breath, hold for two, exhale, and then cry one tear down your left cheek'.

Then there was the infamous milk commercial where I was cast as a young mother. It was a sour pill to swallow for a girl who still considered herself a young ingénue. At least when I saw the commercial I knew they had hired me for my milky white skin and voluptuous bosom, not because I looked mom-ish. When I asked how much the job paid, the casting agent asked me how much I wanted. She ended up taking me into a bathroom stall and handing over an envelope of fifteen hundred kwai, what I asked for. I found out later that the other foreign actors had only asked for a thousand, and the Chinese actors received a flat rate of four hundred.

The commercial started to air right in the midst of the monstrous melamine milk scandal, extensively covered by the international press. Babies were dying of kidney failure because unscrupulous middle management baddies were cutting milk with melamine to raise its protein count and stretch the product to make more money. And that's just when the commercials and billboards with me as 'the face' of milk launched. Lucky me.

CHAPTER 9 – Magic

Norman had meetings all day with a guy named Magic, named for his comprehensive knowledge of the labyrinthine immigration process and his immense guangxi, which allowed him to magically make problems disappear. We were in the process of setting up a WOFE, or Wholly Owned Foreign Enterprise, the first big step towards establishing our business.

From what I understood, this would guarantee Norman and me the coveted Z-Visas instead of our tourist visas, which would allow us to legally live and work in China. Norman had always lived off the radar, but here he felt obligated to be completely transparent, legally speaking, since the consequences in China weren't worth the risk. He had me with him now too, raising the stakes for a once committed bachelor. Already he'd spent days in Magic's office trying to understand the intricacies of owning a business as a foreigner in China.

Nothing was straightforward. For instance, businesses are required to use Bank of China, as the government won't recognize any other banks. There's a cap on how much money can be in a WOFE bank account. A figure originally assumed to be a minimum turned out to be the maximum. And there's a cap on how many employees a WOFE can hire. To do bigger business, which we needed to do or else there wouldn't be a point to any of it, we'd need a larger 'holding company' to sponsor the WOFE. And wouldn't you know? That company had to be Chinese, making the whole 'Wholly Owned Foreign Enterprise' title widely misleading. A joke even, you could say. Not to mention, the Chinese partner all the more powerful and important.

We decided to bring Gage's friend Dougie Brookes on board as our Managing Director. Norman and I could do a lot of things but we needed someone whose sole concern was that of the business, focusing on the hard numbers coming in and going out. He would also oversee the marketing side of things as we got closer to opening. Dougie was young, ambitious and hungry. He said all the right things, had a decent amount of experience, and was happy to put all his weight and enthusiasm behind the project in return for a cut of the action and a high salary once we opened. He wasn't at all a hippie, artist or bohemian, as we considered ourselves to be. He was really into material things, like the highest quality sunglasses, watches and cars. He didn't read or watch movies either, but we took these pedestrian traits as a sign that he'd offer a good balance to what we already brought to the table. And besides, he made us laugh and we liked him.

We had Magic looking into a loophole that would allow Dougie to open a holding company in Hong Kong, alleviating the immediate problem of finding a trustworthy Chinese partner, which was proving difficult. The billionaire movie producer Tino had set us up with had absconded from China with billions and was suspected to be hiding out someplace in Singapore. There was another one of Tino's friends, The Dragon Lady we called her, who was giving us the runaround and wasn't committing, and we began to suspect she never would. Consequently, we were still very much looking. The other benefit of a Hong Kong company is that it's one of the only loopholes that would allow us to filter money out of the country.

I heard Norm's key in the front door and went to welcome him home out of the rain with a towel in hand. He was drenched. After a kiss, I told him there was a warm bath waiting for him. He trotted off, making spit-size puddles on the floor. Wearing my floor-length, sheer, vintage nightgown I shuffled in slippers back into the kitchen to make him a cup of tea and get the sheets out of the drier. Then I waited to hear the latest news from the day, lying on my stomach across the bedroom mattress reading Ellroy's *American Tabloid* for a third time. It was hard to get English books, so I was systematically revisiting my old favorites. Norman finally came out in a bathrobe, laid down on his side of the bed, rubbed his eyes.

"We have that thing tonight, right? Gage's birthday drinks?" he asked.

"Yup! We have to leave here in about an hour and a half." I sat up. "So...? How did it go?"

He groaned, took a deep breath and popped up.

"Let's make the bed... Magic was good. He's a funny guy, I like him. I did all the paperwork, so that's getting sorted. I swear to god darling, the stack of papers was at least five inches thick. The trees... It's all just bullshit too, and you have to sign and stamp every single page. So, basically..."

He stopped and sighed. I sensed there was bad news coming.

"Long story short, there can only be one boss per company and in this case, that has to be me. Magic says they can't put both our names on the licenses. So all this paperwork today was towards the process of making me the boss of the managing company. But then once that is established, we can make you the boss of the operating company, since that has to be a separate company anyways. Don't ask me why. I asked if there was any other way to do it and he said no. There isn't. And you can't ask why because the answer is always, 'This is China'. But this is a problem. It means that I'm about to get legal here, and you're still a long ways off. You have to leave the country every twelve weeks and aren't supposed to be working... and I know I promised you we would be equal partners in this thing, and I want to uphold that promise to you. I need you to feel secure and good about this."

He threw the blanket across the bed for me to tuck in. Even though we'd been together for four years already, his sweetness and consideration towards me was still touching. I smiled at him across the bed, proud to have found one of the good guys out there.

"Magic kept saying that we should just get married, because if we were married none of this stuff would be an issue. As my wife you'd be entitled to half of what's mine, you'd be a resident, be able to work, have a Z-Visa..."

He kept talking, but I was caught up on the 'just get married' part. I heard my voice leave my head saying, "Did you just ask me to marry you?"

"Yes, but I'm afraid you'll say no."

He didn't want to look up at me, a shyness that was almost unrecognizable coming from him, but I couldn't take my eyes off him. I'd never thought of myself as the marrying type, always considered myself the mistress type, but maybe I could... My heart was leaping out of my chest.

"Come over and try me then," I dared. He finally looked at me to read my face. He could see that I was serious. Crazy maybe, but serious.

He went to a drawer, came over and stood in front of me. He started to speak but I told him he'd better get down on one knee and do it properly. In a mixture of laughter and a flash of tears, he popped the question and I said yes. He put a gold wedding band on my finger that was his mother's, and her mother's before that. He said he'd brought to Shanghai 'Just in case'.

He pressed his arm around the small of my back and moved between my legs. Our lips met each other's as if for the first time. Feeling a rush come over me, I pulled my nightgown off over my head and he threw me down on the bed, knowing exactly where to take things from there. He crawled onto the bed as our eyes locked in the reflection of the mirror. He pulled my hair until it hurt and kissed my open mouth. We made love with a kinky tenderness until we couldn't take it anymore. He called me his wife and we came at the same time.

Then we made the bed again.

CHAPTER 10 – Day the Earth Shook

May 12, 2008. There was an earthquake in Sichuan the day we got married. No one really knew the severity of it at the time. Our friends threw us a wedding party where Norman was quick to take credit. He told everyone, 'We got married, went to bed and the earth shook!'

First came a delicious dinner at the famous Beijing Roast Duck restaurant where we were joined by twenty friends. Instead of cutting a wedding cake, we cut the head off a duck. Only in China. Then onto Glamour Bar, where the celebration went into full swing.

The night was perfect, except for one thing. We weren't technically married - we'd been turned down.

Friends of ours got married in Shanghai a few months before we arrived. They told us that it was illegal for two foreign, non-residents to get married in China, but all we had to do was lie and tell our embassies that we were marrying someone Chinese. Then they'd give us the paperwork. After that, we just bring it to the place and they'd marry us. It sounded easy enough.

"Hi! How are you today?" I cheerfully asked the girl behind the desk at the American Embassy. She stared back at me blankly. Right.

"Okay... well, I'm getting married!"

I waited in case she wanted to congratulate me. She didn't.

"So I guess I need to get the paperwork for that? Please?"

"Is your boyfriend Chinese?"

Whoa - she just got straight to it. No mucking about.

"Um, Yeah? Yes! Of course. He's definitely Chinese." I gave her my most earnest, 'Would this face lie to you?' look.

"Fill out the form and come back up to this window when you're done."

After doing my best to keep the facts straight, I returned.

"Norman James Gosney...?" she read out loud. "That is not Chinese name. He is not Chinese."

"Oh, but he is!" I defended right away, feeling my face turning red.

The girl looked at me strangely, then over both shoulders looking for someone to ask. Shit. Here we go. I'd already learned not to expect much from the people behind counters, with their little stamp pads and two-inches of power. Whether it was at the bank or the post office, sometimes it was like dealing with a robot and not an actual, live human being. Maybe that's universal though. I got sent to another window where I paid thirty USD. I thought I'd done it and was damn nearly finished, but then I got asked again to take a seat and wait. When my name was called I stood up confidently. Then I saw who I was going up against. A scrawny, white American guy with glasses and acne. My chest crumbled like the Berlin Wall. I wondered if he'd be able to see right through me. I tried to play it cool and smiled flirtatiously, deciding that this was as good a time as any to take the chopstick out of my long, wavy hair and toss it around like a shampoo commercial.

"Hi there! How are you today?" My Virginia accent comes out strong when I get nervous.

"Fine thanks," he snipped. "You want to marry a Mister… Norman… James… Gosney? Is that correct?"

This guy was for real.

"Yes."

"And he's a Chinese resident I presume?" He looked at me over the top of his glasses. He knew. He had to know. I almost broke. For a second I thought about coming clean in case he trapped me in a lie. Wait, could I go to jail for this? But my head was already nodding nervously.

Then he asked, "How did you two meet?"

Seriously?

"Um, we met here in Shanghai," I lied.

"And why do you want to get married?"

Ha! I laughed out loud at that question. Then cringed. That was probably a completely inappropriate response and I kicked myself for it. It's just a funny question, that's all. One I would've been asking too had I not been the one standing here trying to get a marriage license. I'd never dreamed of a big white wedding and I wasn't even sure I believed in marriage when it came right down to it, but there I was. I wouldn't have considered marrying Norman if

I didn't really love him, so I went with that.

"Because we love each other?"

He peered at me again over his specs, as if he was about to call me a liar to my face, so I added quickly, "And we want to open a business here together."

That he bought. He slid a Bible through the hole in the Plexiglas and asked me to place my right hand on it and raise my left hand. I couldn't believe these archaic rituals still existed. I almost told him that I'm an Atheist, but I bit my tongue.

"Do you swear that all the information you've provided here is the truth?"

"Absolutely," I said, feeling most unscrupulous. Then he gave me a one page, one paragraph, chopped and signed letter that said The United States of America approved of my marriage to Norman James Gosney, resident of China.

At the British Embassy they didn't question whether or not Amelia Boswell Kallman was in fact Chinese, but they did charge Norman the equivalent of three hundred GBP for his paperwork. He was also informed of the medieval British tradition of Posting the Bans. Originally it meant nailing a marriage announcement to the local church door for twenty days prior to the wedding for the perusal, and possible disapproval, of all interested parties. Here it was to be thumbtacked to a bulletin board in a hallway. He tried to explain to the woman behind the counter that the likelihood of anyone we knew walking by a bulletin board in the back of the UK embassy in Shanghai China, recognizing our names, and then objecting to our marriage seemed highly bloody unlikely, but he was told 'Those are the rules' and sent on his way.

When the wedding day eventually came, we asked Gage to come along as our witness. He was dressed sharp in a white linen summer suit. Norman sported a full morning suit with vest, spats and tie, and a long coat, most dapper. I wore my white and silver movie star dress from Trash and Vaudeville on St. Marks that came down just past me knees. Gathered around the waist, it sat low on my cleavage and was held up by spaghetti straps that fell teasingly off my shoulders. Letting my tender years shine through, I wore hardly any make-up, my grandmother's white beaded gloves and leopard print pumps. Oddly calm, I wasn't experiencing any of the fabled symptoms expected in brides-to-be. I figured it's because, once I set my mind to something, I don't look back. For better or worse.

Telling my parents was the most nerve-racking part. I'm very lucky to have wonderful, supportive, hard-working parents who gave me an excellent example of a happy, healthy partnership. My mom was still mad at me over the whole moving-to-China thing though. My dad supported that decision, but I wasn't really sure how they were going to take the news that their youngest daughter was eloping with a man who was closer to their age than hers.

Using Skype, I called them. Just hearing their voices made it harder. This must be the part of the wedding day that really gets people, I thought. The agony of the moment, I could feel it in my belly. I said it quickly, like pulling off a Band-Aid. I said something to the effect of:

"Hi guys. I've got great news. I'm getting married... Today!"

The suspended silence that followed was broken by the sound of my mother crying. My dad offered mild congratulations. My mom asked me if I was sure. When I hung up, my heart felt like a rock situated amongst a shallow cold spring, clogging up my throat. Like I'd just aged ten years. When I walked into the kitchen where Norman waited with Gage, the air disappeared as we took in the seriousness of what was about to go down.

We got out of a taxi in Gubei in front of what appeared to be a convention center. Gage took our picture in front of a massive billboard of the famous Shanghai skyline under a banner that read 'Renewable Energy Benefit All People.' We took the elevator to the tenth floor. I was tap dancing, Norm was singing, Gage was snapping photos. The elevator door opened. We walked out to a sign that read MARRIAGE, with an arrow pointing left, and DIVORCE, with an arrow pointing right. We laughed self-consciously and carried on, squinting in the florescent lit hallway that led to a baby-pink room with grey linoleum floors. Not exactly how I'd pictured my small, skinny Chinese wedding.

"Why do I get the feeling we've just walked into a bad David Lynch movie?" I remarked.

"One that needs subtitles," Norman joked.

The wedding factory looked like The Communist Party meets 1985 high-school prom. There was an arch of very fake pink and purple plastic flowers and a matching arch of deflating pink and white balloons. There's a photo-shopped backdrop of a Tudor style castle through fall leaves. Next to that, three racks of outlandish, whimsical, highly embellished rentable gowns. The photographer leaning over one of the racks looked to be asleep except for a lit cigarette that hung out his mouth, ashes falling on his sleeves.

We approached the desk in the far corner, handed over our paperwork and waited, holding hands, completely smitten. A constipated, scowling woman took our papers and went into the backroom. Minutes later she resurfaced with a waddling, shorthaired woman who handed our papers back saying that we couldn't get married because I was missing a sentence from my paperwork.

I guess this was the point when they realized that neither of us were Chinese.

I tried tears, Norman tried charm and in a best effort, Gage tried to slip her three hundred kwai, but she wasn't having it. I'd have to go back to my embassy and get the sentence added. Period. And by the time I could go to my embassy and get back, the wedding factory would be closed, and it wouldn't be open again for two whole days. Our wedding day was officially ruined.

Before we left Gage snuck us into the chapel and shot our only wedding photos amongst the Chinese flag, fake plastic flower bouquets and Mao's *The Little Red Book*. We did our best impressions of how two people who just got married might look.

"Hey," Norman said, turning my chin to meet his eyes. "Today I married you in my heart."

Two days later we marched into the convention center as New Yorkers, ready for a fight. I handed over my revised paragraph. This time there wasn't a problem. The whole thing lasted maybe ten minutes. We were asked the regular, 'Do you promise to look after each other in sickness and in health,' but we hadn't expected the final questions.

"Do you promise you aren't related?"

Um... Yeah... Gross.

And, "Do you promise to take care of each other's parents until they die?'

Sorry, what? We stopped and looked at each other confirming we'd heard that right.

"My parents are dead," Norman told the woman.

I jabbed him in the ribs and we both said, 'I do'. And with that we were handed two red, passport-like certificates that said, in Chinese, that we were officially and legally married.

That night I wanted to go out for a drink to celebrate, just the two of us. I thought we'd check out the new Chinese nightclub that opened around the corner from our apartment. I'd been to a few of the Chinese mega-clubs, like MT, pronounced 'empty', rumored to be a Westerner's revenge. My favorite was Babyface. At these spots, I attracted an instant fan club. Short, smiley, black hair, rhythmless dancing boys circled around me with pointy-finger dance moves, chuckling every time they got too close and accidently brushed the back of their pointy- finger hands against my tits. As if I wouldn't notice.

This evening the club happened to be holding a fundraiser for Sichuan Earthquake Relief. It was reported in the international press that the government had been warned a week prior that an earthquake was likely to occur at that time in Sichuan, but they chose to ignore the prediction and failed to alert the village. The death toll was still escalating in the thousands. The majority of fatalities were children, victims of badly constructed schools thought to be the direct consequence of corruption and bribery.

We walked through the tunnel lobby into the thumping club. The impact of the booming bass and the zooming pink laser-beams stopped me in my tracks. The place was packed with locals. We fought our way through the dancing hoards looking for the bar. Norman touched my arm and pointed up. News footage from Sichuan was being projected all around us. The bloody dead children, the grieving, sobbing mothers and the body parts being pulled from the rubble... Everywhere we looked. I thought I must be dreaming. I turned around and saw go-go dancers, gyrating their hips on tabletops, dressed as sexy angels. Was that supposed to be ironic? What kind of a sick joke was this? Too soon maybe? Without saying a word, we took one look at each other and left, the urge to celebrate dampened.

As we silently walked home in the starless night I could feel it. I'd crossed a line. I was no longer a tourist, awestruck by sensory stimulation and the weird incongruities of a culture I so wanted to love. The veneer was lifted. The gloss was gone. I'd become a resident of The People's Republic. I'd achieved a real sense of China, not just what foreigners think they see after a few weeks or months here when they see what they want to. Now I was seeing things I didn't want to.

I guess I don't understand communism. I thought it meant having a classless society, where people have common ownership and work together for the greater good. But I don't think China's that way at all. If anything it seems more like fascism to me. The people are basically controlled by a totalitarian government, a class one must be born into. The people in charge are willing to do anything to remain in power and make sure the people below have nowhere to rise.

In a way I think this creates the opposite values of those intended by communism. Instead of participating in and looking out for the whole of society, people have become selfish, greedy and protective of what they do have. The ones who question authority or don't conform to walk in step are punished. This results in a population who have become robotic and easy-to-herd, brainwashed. Someone told me that there is no direct translation for the word *politics* in Chinese, depriving people of even the basic language to think about such things for themselves.

This won't last though. It can't. As the gap between rich and poor increases, so does the bitter jealousy of the lower class. While the government can resist inflation tooth and nail, it can't resist forever. And there lies the potential root for discord, uprising and dare I say, revolution in China. Made all the more possible and likely by the government's greatest nemesis: Pandora's Box, otherwise known as the internet. Citizens have access to information now like never before. Repressed voices have a forum to be heard, not just by their local village, but also by the whole world.

There was an underline sense of controversy and hostility percolating up from the streets. Like it was just a matter of time...

It had taken me awhile, but now I had finally grasped just what a huge idea it was to bring burlesque to China. It was impossible and crazy, and maybe even defiantly naïve, but now that we fully understood the great wall of challenges we were up against, and how far we had already come just through sheer persistence, we knew that there was no turning back. This project

was bigger than all of us, and came to mean more -
to ourselves, to the expat community, to Shanghai, and
even the Chinese government - than we had ever
imagined possible. Pulling off Chinatown meant
pulling off a miracle, and that's what we intended to
do.

PART 2:

PULLING OFF A MIRACLE

CHAPTER 11 – Auditions

Finding himself between apartments, we invited Dougie to stay in our guestroom until he found another place. Sometimes it felt like Norman and I were playing house and Dougie was our overgrown teenage son. In other ways, he was like a brother, becoming a close friend and confidante to both me and Norman. Apartment 2B had a constant rhythm of laughter, music, love, the comings and goings of friends, late night waves of inspiration, necessary arguments, and some poignant shared life moments. The death of Dougie's grandfather, followed closely by the death of mine, bonded us intimately. Being so far away from our families, we became each other's family. The best times were when Dougie would get me laughing, usually over something Norman said or did that struck his funny bone. We'd both end up in hysterical, bellyaching conniptions on the floor, tears rolling down our cheeks, unable to speak, like being tickled to death. The more Norman pretended to be annoyed, the more we laughed. Not many people have ever made me crack up that hard.

We sat at a long table waiting for auditions to begin: Dougie, Star, Norman and me. Dougie was taking a real shine to Star, even though she had a Chinese boyfriend since high-school and would likely marry him since their families had already agreed to the arrangement. Dougie put his foot in his mouth when he daftly asked her if she had any brothers or sisters. Her generation doesn't have brothers or sisters. She kindly ignored his faux pas and told us about her cousin who she calls sister. Star's English failed her sometimes, but she made up for it with cuteness and animated determination to express herself. I'd be staring into her purple eyes, nodding and smiling with encouragement, even if I didn't have a clue what she was on about. I made her my Dance Captain and invited her to sit in on the audition panel with us, interpreting as needed.

I promoted our general auditions for weeks, but the response was underwhelming. I feared that we weren't going to be able to find the talent we needed. Less than twenty people made appointments, which seemed low to me considering all the English and Chinese publicity I'd done online, at dance studios, in the papers and at a bizarre performing arts college that had been like a Twilight Zone episode. In the student lounge every wall was blank. Glaringly empty. It looked like a mental institution for zombies. Creepy quiet, no one speaking. No one sat in groups, no guitars, no eccentrics. I think performing arts college, I think weirdoes, pot-heads, rebels, bad haircuts, day drinking... Pretty people at least. This was not that. It was queer. I posted a flyer up quickly, guerilla-style, then got the hell out of there as fast as I could.

I decided to name our chorus line The Chinatown Dolls. Unlike the Moulin Rouge, we want each girl in the line to have a unique look, like the United Nations of Showgirls, with someone for everyone to fall in love with. That being said, I prepared myself for the fact that I might have to take what I could get.

Kayla was on time and volunteered to go first. I liked her already. Wearing a tight aqua blue t-shirt that showed off her midriff, I could see the top of a flower tattoo sunk below her white short-shorts. About 5'4" with brown shoulder length hair she had a square jaw, big Bambi, come-hither eyes, and a touch of baby-fat that gave her dimples. She exuded an overall effect of being gorgeous, exotic and young. A saucy piece of jailbait. She held the center of the room, closed her eyes and sang an a capella rendition of Christina Aguilera's 'Impossible'. A perfectly pitched gospel voice soared out of the pretty chanteuse. The hair on the back of my neck stood up.

When she finished, Norman and I exchanged a promising look. I asked her where she studied, and she replied, 'In the shower. I'm self-taught'. Originally from a Muslim family in Tashkent, Uzbekistan, she'd been living by herself in Shanghai for two years. She was nineteen.

"I saw the audition notice on Smartshanghai.com and I liked the description. I've sung a lot here, but all the gigs are... not very classy. I'm ready for a change."

I knew then that I wanted to work with her. She had spunk and reminded me of myself only a few years ago. She also couldn't wait to dance as a showgirl in the chorus line and get her kit off doing burlesque. She went on to show us part of a bellydance routine she was working on. We hired her on the spot.

Several locals came through, giving me some satisfaction that all my translated promotion wasn't in vain. Admittedly, one was only interested in working in the kitchen, and another played the drums so he couldn't audition really because there wasn't a drum kit. Another local guy wore headphones and proceeded to dance for us, throwing spastic shapes unlike any moves I'd ever seen, but not in a good way. It was tough to keep a straight face when Star launched into him in Shanghainese, telling him he wasn't a good dancer and that he needed to go back and take classes.

A good-looking blonde, blue-eyed Australian, Benny from Brisbane, auditioned with a Dean Martin song. Afterwards he told us he had degrees in both theatre and Chinese, and had always hoped that something like Chinatown would come along. His potential was clear. Having a fluent Chinese speaking lǎowài who could sing classic jazz standards in Chinese as well as act in character parts could only be a good thing. Norman had him pegged for '2nd Banana'.

The auditions concluded with three leggy dancers who came in all at once. Pinky was Shanghainese and kind of sexy despite keeping her lips tightly pulled over braces. The other two were Russian girls, Natasha and Irene. Natasha smiled, at least vaguely. She had long blond hair pulled into a tight ponytail. Her face was plain but I imagined it would paint up nicely. Irene didn't smile once. She had that hard Russian look that made her appear old despite her youth. A caricature of the classic Russian dancer type, the kind Norman and I dreaded ending up with a chorus line full of.

"They're really great looking girls with amazing tight bods," Norman would confide privately. "But they're miserable people to work with. They dance blankly with no soul, no passion, like, 'You pay me money, then maybe I dance for you."

They performed an acrobatic, hip-hop inspired routine before taking turns dancing solos. They showed off their best moves, with kicks straight up in the air down into the splits. Pinky was the best of the three, but I decided to invite all of them to train since it didn't look like I was in any danger of having too many dancing girls.

We did two more days of auditions through a Chinese talent agency. I wasn't sure what to expect when Norman, Dougie and I were dropped off in Gubei in front of a miniature, tackier version of Las Vegas' Caesar's Palace. It had gold painted lions on either side of the entrance, pissing cherubs, hollow plastic columns covered in fake ivy, and a dozen plastic palm-trees. The further one gets from the center of Shanghai, the more one is treated to jaw-dropping examples of kitsch, and sheer 'Oh my gosh, how could they' bad taste.

The first day we saw fifteen acts, and on the second we saw ten. Except for two magicians the rest of the acts were children. I'd made it clear to the agent that we were an adult nightclub so it hadn't occurred to me that we would be auditioning kids.

Every act we saw was a standard Chinese circus act and it didn't take long to learn that there are only about eight different acts. Every kid or group of kids did slight variations of the exact same routine. They wore pink, blue or yellow lycra jumpsuits with sequined V's in a complimentary color framing their necks, like Star Trek meets Chinese disco. The music was a mash-up of ethnic Han meets bubblegum meets electro-pop drum machine. After the first few acts we were already looking at each other thinking *this is going to be a long day*. When I asked the agent why she didn't have more adult acts, she explained that adults don't perform on stage because they're too old to do the routines. Fair enough.

We saw teams of tiny, pre-pubescent boys juggling straw hats, and slightly older boys dressed in Chinese Opera costumes with masks rigged to instantaneously change faces when they made a certain gesture. Every time we saw that act the masks got stuck in between two of the faces, ruining the magic and ending the act right then and there. No amount of stagecraft can save you from that caliber of a technical error, and we couldn't afford to risk such a malfunction on a nightly basis. Itty-bitty, Jon-Benet-styled girls in bright blue eye-shadow, rouge and pink lipstick, who couldn't have been older than seven or eight, did acts where they bite down onto a free standing mouthpiece that supports their contorting bodies off the ground in striking, mind-boggling, sexualized positions. The little girls were really skilled at what they did, but the over all effect left us feeling slightly ill. There was no way we could put that on stage in a nightclub. I made a point to show approval to the young performers, clapping and smiling for every act. I'd tell them in Chinese that they were very good or very beautiful, and thanked them for entertaining me.

The next age group of the girls specialized in balancing a glass of water on top of a fan, on top of another fan balanced on chins. They could toss and spin umbrellas in the air with their feet and balance five fully lit candelabras on their bodies as they did a three-sixty turn on the floor, which was impressive. The magic acts centered around drugged doves squeezed into tight places. And finally, there was a truly dangerous roller-skating act where one of the older girls spun around in tight circles on skates, connected to a tiny girl by a mouthpiece they shared, clenched between teeth. The little one spun, flying through the air until her body was horizontal to the ground, orbiting the older girl in dizzying circles. That one left us holding onto each other with sweaty palms. It would be way too stressful on us to have to watch that act every night, let alone an audience.

The only act that I was really interested in for Chinatown was these two adorable seven-year-old twin boys who performed a hat-juggling act. Mischievous and competitive, they performed with a brotherly spirit, bringing something more to their act than the others. It was reminiscent of old vaudeville. They had show business. And sadly, they were one of the only acts that looked like they actually enjoyed performing. To put their routine on our stage I wanted to costume them in matching mini-tuxedos and have them juggling top hats to 'Puttin' on the Ritz'. It could be a showstopper!

When the two days were over, I felt haunted by the glimpse into these children's lives. They lived at their school, under a teacher's care, practicing routines instead of academics. Most of their careers would be over in their late teens, their bodies prematurely aged from brutal conditioning. I heard that they even break baby's hips purposefully so they are more flexible as they grow so that they can have a career in contortion.

One of the smallest contortionists forgot to loop the elastic over her feet, which was meant to keep the pant legs secure when she kicked her legs into the air. When she was upside-down the pants fell to her knees, revealing bruises in shades of green, purple and brown, over-lapping on every inch of her feet and shins.

I left feeling more alarmed than entertained. Like I wanted to do something to help them, and I questioned what an appropriate role, if any, I could play in some of these children's lives. On the one hand, they were going to be working one way or another and if they were working for me, then at least I'd ensure that they'd be well looked after in a safe environment. But on the other hand, if we hired them, would we be showing our implied support of this kind of institution? One that felt dangerously close to the realm of child exploitation and abuse.

I started performing professionally when I was just a kid and even then, nothing gave me greater pleasure than being on stage in front of an applauding audience. I wondered if this kind of school would've appealed to me. If I had been born Chinese, would this be my life? While I hoped that some of the kids were enjoying themselves, it was apparent that for many their reasons for being there had nothing to do with a passion for performing. It was commerce. Tiny wage earners for families poorer than I could imagine.

CHAPTER 12 – Party City

After auditions Norman and I rushed off to change clothes for an evening out. There was a seven course, matched wine meal waiting for us at the highest restaurant in the world, the yet to be opened Shanghai World Financial Center. Shanghai was affirming itself as the party capital of the Eastern world. I expected that in leaving New York my days of endless nights and over-indulgence would be kept to a minimum, but Shanghai was out to prove me wrong. Every night of the week there was a party going on or an occasion to celebrate. Everything had a 'once in a lifetime' feel about it, reminding me that these really were the good old days. And I loved always having an excuse to dress up in my finest vintage glamour and fabric market fashions.

Shanghai was full of suited expats - people who work for big corporations, nine to five. Being creative types embarking on such a daring project, we were propelled to the top of the social ladder and found ourselves in high demand. Connected by our foreignness, I got to hang out with Talib Kwali, Fab 5

Freddy, DJ Sasha and other celebrities passing through town, as if we were old mates. It wasn't uncommon to go from a dinner party, to a gallery opening, to a fashion party, to a jazz club, to a dive bar, before ending up at one of the infamous afterhours clubs dancing until nine in the morning.

Shanghai's also a city for unapologetic networking. You don't go anywhere without business cards in hand. Our network of friends and acquaintances was more varied than it was in Manhattan. Maybe it's because expats don't have roots or family there, or because people come and go so frequently. There's a great diversity of quality, interesting people on the scene. Everyone got themselves to Shanghai somehow and everyone had a story, a dream they were chasing or something they were running away from. Misfit foreigners afloat on a sprawling sea of Chinese. This commonality unified people from all over the world in a great social experiment that defined the era. The downside was that it could feel like a rather small, gossipy village at times. Everyone knew each other's business, fucked the same people and went to the same clubs, making the potential for catty claws and jealous jowls tangible.

We made friends with another power-couple: British-born August Helm, famous for opening Hong Kong's Canton Disco in the '80's, the first modern nightclub in what has become the city's party district, Lan Kwai Fong; And his wife, Julie Helm, a former Miss Hong Kong and the first Chinese woman to pose for Playboy. She still looked incredible. They owned a party bus that chauffeured our crew around the city between parties. The bus became our own private VIP room, as it was fully equipped with a DJ booth, stripper's pole and a stocked bar. Drugs were everywhere if you wanted them. Ecstasy, cocaine, acid, Special K, MDMA, hashish, you name it. And it was just handed out, free of charge. No one worried about the police.

One night August introduced me to a pole-dancer he hired to perform on the bus. Her name was Josephine, of Chinese decent but from Australia. Short with a boxy, muscular frame, there was something very coquettish about her, like she was trying to master the art of being a Geisha. The way she batted her eyes, the way she laughed... I could see her making a good showgirl. We exchanged business cards, and then she climbed back up the pole, showing off her best moves.

I made friends with a couple of lǎowài deejays and together we started to host Mod Dance Parties once a month at Logo. Back in New York, I used to be in two rock bands: The Countess and the C.U.N.T. Rock Revolution and The Smith Island Asylum. Don't get me wrong, I don't claim to have any real musical talent to speak of, but I throw myself at the music, punk rock-style. I can sing back-up, play the tambourine and the kazoo, beat box on the mic, rock out in a showgirl costume, interpret songs in American Sign Language, and just generally be a bad ass. I loved every second of getting to pretend I was some kind of rock star. So in a way the Mod Dance Parties filled that hole in my life.

I was the dancer-mascot in a short, white Twiggy dress and go-go boots, styled like Amy Winehouse. As the boys would spin, I'd dance my little butt off for five hours straight. It put me right in the center of Shanghai's virgin underground rock scene. When Beijing's number one rock band, New Pants, 'The Chinese Ramones', came to town, they had heard of me and I was hired to be their dancer on the Shanghai leg of their tour.

On weekends we ventured outside of the city for short holidays with friends. We went to the mountains of Moganshan to see the bamboo forests, to breath in less-polluted air and splash in waterfalls with abandon. We took a ferry out to Chong Ming Island, which claimed to be in the process of becoming the first 'green' island. It was also the home for the planned Chinese Disneyland and a reconstruction of Michael Jackson's home, Neverland, so his fans wouldn't have to pilgrimage all the way to America to pay homage to the King of Pop. There I took acid for the first time in a national forest. I became acutely aware that every inch of grass was cut at exactly two inches, and every tree was planted exactly one meter apart. It was most unnatural, especially on acid. There was a sign that urged people not to get into the paddleboats, 'If you are pregnant or a zombie'.

We visited Thames Town, an area just outside of Shanghai that's modeled to resemble an English city, so when Brits come they won't feel homesick. Hired Chinese actors dress in badly copied Edwardian garb, walk up and down the empty streets with no Brits, or anyone for that matter, in sight. Then there was the Kunming Dwarf Village where the little people live in large mushroom houses and wear costumes of characters from fairytales, marketing their town as a small tourist attraction.

While on these trips I appreciated the fresher air and the night skies, I found the outskirts fairly dreary, dismal and depressed, and was always happy to return to the city. My city. Shanghai had become my home.

CHAPTER 13 – Tits Out

It had been over a year already and while Tino, Norman's former New York business partner and the guy who originally encouraged us to come to Shanghai, had been helpful in setting up a couple of meetings from abroad, he still hadn't been over to visit. Finally, Norman got a call from him. He had news. Bad news. The federal and state police made over fifty arrests in connection to organized crime and the New Jersey sport's book, one of the biggest busts in recent times. He sent his deepest apologies on behalf of his close associates, but there was no way they were going to be able to fund Chinatown anymore... Too much trouble at home.

We held an emergency meeting, Norman, Dougie and me. We had already invested much of our personal finances into securing the venue, setting up the business, bribery, and moving our lives to China. We agreed that giving up and accepting our losses was not an option. We had to keep moving forward. There was no Plan B. Anyways, the project was too good and had too much momentum behind it to quit now.

Everyone in Shanghai was anticipating the birth of Chinatown. We were here to make history, not just open a good nightclub. We wanted Chinatown to be legendary. A club that would be referred to in the future in the same tone as Studio 54, Limelight and CBGB's.

It was time to test our personal guangxi. Dougie had hopeful connections in Australian real estate, and Norman would press Tino to facilitate electronic introductions to his other rich Chinese friends. We'd put the word out that we were in the market for a large partner, as well as offering individual shares to people who believed in the project and wanted to be involved.

Norman and Dougie were working so hard to make this dream a reality and I could see how much these setbacks stressed them out. I wanted to help, but wasn't sure what I could do besides be a pillar of positivity and support. Then it dawned on me that I could do what I do best: Throw a party! We could use it to showcase what a night at Chinatown might offer and gain awareness that we were in the market for a partner.

When we first began this project we'd been warned of jealous club owners making trouble for new venues, so to avoid this we courted and consulted several established Chinese club and restaurant owners. We schmoozed them with the intention of giving them face and getting their blessings on our venture. We were doing everything we could to make sure we didn't get screwed and end up just another Shanghai cliché. It was during that time when we met Len, the Chinese owner of the highly successful jazz club, JZ. He understood that while we intended to have some live music, we were not attempting to go into competition with him, and underlined that there was potential for our venues to assist each other when it came to booking international acts, getting performance visas, and things like that.

I gave Len a call, explained our situation and asked if we could put on an event at his place. A One-Night-Only featuring our singer from New York, Freddy Fontaine, with the JZ Big Band. We made a deal for a Saturday night and he offered me a fair promoter's deal on the door. I was on a roll, getting a charge from talking Club Owner to Club Owner when I heard my big mouth say, 'And you don't mind if I do a quick burlesque that night, do you?' He said that would be fine, though I have a feeling he didn't know what burlesque actually meant, but didn't want to admit it.

After I hung up it hit me like a salty ocean wave breaking in my face: What had I just done? I was going to do *burlesque*? Here's the thing: While I've had tons of experience prancing around in feathers and performing 'Any Movie in 3-Minutes', I'd never actually done real burlesque in the traditional sense of the word before. And everyone would be looking at me, the said expert, the showgirl from New York there to bring burlesque to Shanghai. I'd have to set an example and act like I knew what I was doing.

I asked Norman if he thought that we could get away with doing burlesque at the event, legally speaking, and said that if it was just the one act, one time, he didn't think it would be a problem. Then I informed him of my plan. I put on an air of confidence, slipping it into the conversation like it was no big deal.

"You? You can't do it," he said. "You can't do it... Unless you do something really exceptional that blows people away. Everyone's going to judge us on this, you know. It'll make or break us. You can't do it unless you are one hundred percent sure that you're going to get it right."

"Well, I'll just have to get it right then, won't I?" Now I couldn't back down. Telling me I can't do something just makes me more determined to do it.

"Yeah. You do. And you're not going to get your tits out, right?"

"No," I pouted.

Norman and I are both stubborn people and we only ever argue over artistic differences. When we first started working together I was pursuing a professional acting career and he made me swear that if I got into business with him that I wouldn't go topless. He didn't want to be the guy who turned his girlfriend into a stripper. He said I had too much talent, and while I have an awesome rack, 'Once you pop your tits out, you can't pop 'em back in'. Ultimately it was my decision though. I love my Double D's, and have been known to flash them on occasion. It would be selfish not to. When I was sixteen my boyfriend brought me to a Hell's Angels party in Culpepper, Virginia, where I won a hundred dollars in a wet t-shirt contest. So it's not like I'm shy. But when it came right down to it, I still couldn't help but consider my lineage of Christian ministers and my church-going mother saying, 'I'll be happy with whatever you decide to do, as long as you don't become a stripper'. Sort of ironic now that I think about it. If she found out, she would kill me- literally. Wearing a bikini-like outfit was one thing, people wear less on the beach, but full on nudity? Obviously I'd go straight to hell. Photos could wind up on the internet... No - I'd come this far with most of my clothes on, I'd have to come up with a way to do burlesque that was still sexy and satisfying, but didn't end in tassels. Maybe I hadn't really thought this through. I wondered if I could train one of my new showgirls to do a routine. Maybe they'd be up for getting their tits out?

Wait a minute. What was I thinking? The original intention of burlesque was political parody and satire. It wasn't all about exposing breasts, that didn't come until much later. This could be my chance to redefine burlesque, on my own terms. I could make up an act that was sexy and filthy without going down to pasties and a g-string. Might even be sexier leaving some things to the imagination. I had the chance to do something really original and clever, something that was mine, my mark on this world. It would be a challenge, but hey, I like a challenge.

CHAPTER 14 – All That Jazz

What started as a small idea to give potential investors a glimpse of what they would be investing in, quickly turned into a much bigger deal when SmartShanghai.com posted the event. Announcing it as the first burlesque performance in China, they called it, 'The party everyone is talking about'. When the night came, no one blinked at the one hundred-kwai cover charge, and a line formed around the block. All our friends piled into the second floor balcony of the small rectangular hall and before we knew it, the club had to turn people away for the first time in history. Dougie and Norman organized themselves at a table with serious potential Chinese investors to be entertained with the expected fruit platters, green tea whisky, and champagne at Chinatown's expense, in hopes that one of them would take the bait.

Star and Kayla were costumed like Vegas showgirls. I made Star her very own costume from scratch since there was no way her almost non-existent breasts could do justice to one of my bejeweled tops. Her costume was purple, pink and gold, constructed for less than thirty USD. I also bought her a long brown wig with bangs, changing her whole look from boyish gamine into a feminine beauty queen. Kayla was able to artificially pad out the red, orange and gold top that was my very first showgirl costume from New York, and she wore a long, bright red wig that she bought especially for the occasion.

"Okay. Just remember ladies, have fun! You girls look gorgeous! And the idea is to let people know about the club and the shows. You can mention that there are still investment opportunities available, and if someone asks you questions about it or seems interested, introduce them to Norman or Dougie. Cool? Oh, and if anyone gives you are hard time just be a bitch. You have my full permission. Or tell Dougie or Norman and they'll take care of it, okay? But I don't think you'll have any problems in this crowd. Are you nervous?"

"I'm not nervous," Kayla declared, posing for herself in the mirror. "I hope my ex comes tonight and sees me, he's going to be so jealous!"

I began to change into a long, silver sequined gown. Star stood directly in front of me in the cramped bathroom and complained in her high-pitched voice.

"I have no boobs! I wish I had your boobs. They are so beautiful. May I touch please?"

It wasn't the first time a Chinese girl had asked to touch my tits, and I always thought it was funny how upfront and curious they were about it. Standing up straight and pulling my straps down, fully exposing my peaches, Star got a ravenous look in her eyes and I braced myself for an attack. Instead she laid my tits gently in her palms, bouncing them a bit, and then rubbed her thumbs over my nipples, causing a reaction that made it feel more dangerous than I was prepared for.

"Okay, that's enough." We giggled together for a second and I adjusted myself back into the dress. "I need a drink."

As I came down the stairs, my eyes locked with Freddy Fontaine's. My lips curled as I strutted up next to him at the bar, deliberately ignoring him in a flirty game.

"Come here often?" he said, not missing a beat. He turned to me suavely in his tuxedo, looking like a debonair movie star with dazzling brown eyes, chiseled features and a shaved bald head.

"I hear there is a singer performing here tonight who is supposed to be kind of okay."

"Kind of okay?" He had dimples when he smiled. "Well I hear there is some showgirl here tonight doing the first burlesque in Shanghai and you know what? I suspect this might be her first time ever doing a burlesque routine," he teased taking a sip of his double whiskey on the rocks and reveling in that bit of insider information that cut straight through me. I took the glass out of his hand and put it to my lips, throwing it back, indulging in the warm sting of whiskey down my throat, before setting it down noisily on the bar.

"Well I need it more than you do then, huh?"

Freddy had no choice but to laugh in his deep, Southern style. It was good to be in the company of an old friend, someone who knew me from times and places that people in Shanghai would never understand. There was something about standing together at a bar on the opposite side of the world from where we first met that made our reunion all the more exhilarating. His presence brought an easy confidence.

Together, between me, him and Norman, we knew that even if disaster was to strike we would still be able to pull off an impressive show based purely on our raw talents. Because that's who we are, and that's what we do.

A bit rough around the edges, Freddy's a cowboy type who speaks and moves at the speed of a horse trot. Originally from Tulsa, Oklahoma, he had the good sense to escape to New York as soon as he could. It's a mystery why he isn't a bigger star. He has it all: The looks, voice, chops, drive. But I can't complain because it means he's our star. It appeared that his third marriage had hit a rough patch and the timing of working in the Orient had proven a well-timed vacation. At fifty, he was in the best shape of his life, doing a thousand sit-ups a day, claiming it helped his diaphragm and that his voice had never sounded better.

When we were getting ready to start our speakeasy in New York, Norman was beside himself at the thought of doing shows without Freddy, who had moved to Hawaii for a couple of years with his wife and kids. I got sick of hearing him say, 'Damn, I wish Freddy was here, I don't want to do a show without Freddy', so I had gone ahead and set up auditions for three guys to fill Freddy's shoes, when there was a knock at the door. By some miracle, there stood Freddy Fontaine asking when he could get back up on stage. That's what I call good timing. The first time I heard him sing I understood what the big deal was. He sings Sinatra better than Sinatra did on his best nights. He knows every song in the American songbook and even has Sinatra's entire original, hard-to-get backing tracks by Nelson Riddle, as well as one of Old Blue Eyes' microphones from The Sands.

Always a professional, Freddy made us look good and in return, we made him look good and promised to make him a star in China. His one request was that he got to share a dressing room with the showgirls, something he would often remind us with a cheeky grin. Even though he was a southern gentleman at heart, he did enjoy the occasional benefits, the perks if you will, of the profession. I only had to watch him to make sure that he didn't drink too much whiskey before a show, and that he didn't throw any punches after the whiskey, after the show, but even these attributes were part of his endearing crooner persona.

Norman introduced Freddy to the stage in front of the JZ Big Band as 'The world's greatest living lounge singer', and from the way Freddy worked that crowd - strutting across the stage, flirting with the audience, showing off his dance moves - no one doubted it. He had the audience eating out of the palm of his hand in no time. His voice swam over the instruments into the bellies of the audience like comfort food, melting like butter on the roof of the mouth. Looking around, I could see the women in the audience sipping straws knowingly and wiggling their hips, wondering if he was single. The men looked to be enjoying the familiar tunes too. Freddy always came across like a guy you would like to have a cold beer with, but someone you shouldn't leave alone with your girlfriend for too long. By the end of the first set everyone was raving and festively drinking, starting to get a bit rowdy. I made my way to the bathroom to get ready for my first burlesque.

"This is going great!" Dougie exclaimed. "Did you see? Jack Benson and Rob Lee are here!"

We both laughed. Jack Benson, an ancient white-haired expat, lived off the credential of being in the first Bruce Lee movie and would show up to the opening of an envelope if they served free booze. Rob Lee was a local weirdo who was always offering his unsolicited opinions and claiming to have many famous friends, though he was always mysteriously alone. Both had established themselves as markers by which a party could be judged, Warhol style, and it wasn't *the* party in Shanghai unless these two old letches were there.

My Shanghai debut would be an act I called, 'The Bride of Frankenstein', performed to the original movie theme, a moody masterpiece by the legendary Max Steiner. It was inspired by an old vaudeville routine I came across. A photo of a woman who disguises half her body as the devil, with his fake head attached to her shoulder and her right arm becomes his. She carries on a scene interacting with him, making it look like two people are on stage, not just one. I was attracted to the possibilities of this dynamic, especially because it played to my strengths as an actress. We designed a head out of papier-mâché to start experimenting with, and Norman fabricated the complicated, Victorian-looking device that attached the head to my body, allowing me to disrobe while maintaining the illusion and not revealing the mechanics.

I knew that whatever I wore in the act, it had to come off easily with just one hand, so I made an old, white stained tablecloth into a hospital gown that tied like the authentic Bedlam item, in three bows. Easy for 'Dr. Frankenstein' to take off of me, revealing my Bride of Frankenstein body in a white bra, knickers, garter belt and stockings. A black afro wig was made into a cone with white zigzag streaks sewn up the sides, and one curl pulled out over my forehead, an Elsa Lancaster meets sexy Elvis effect. My puppet had a crazy-professor wig, bald on the top with gray hair shooting out the sides and his 'other hand' pinned over my shoulder, draped black velvet creating the illusion of his body.

Norman came into the bathroom to help me with my final preparations.

"Are you nervous? Don't be nervous," he spoke firmly as a boss, not my husband.

"Yup," I said.

It was not so much stage fright. I'm a pro at focusing my energy and turning it into adrenaline. But rather I felt the weight of our future on my shoulders. I couldn't afford to mess this up.

"You'll be great," he told me, giving the costume a final once over. "It looks unbelievably real. I got jealous earlier watching you rehearse. I don't like to see some other bloke touching up my missus. Just get out there and show them what you're made of. You'll blow them away."

He's my biggest, yet most critical fan, but I wouldn't have it any other way.

Dougie and Norman surrounded me with a giant tablecloth so I could be transported to the center of the curtainless stage for the necessary dramatic 'reveal'. Dougie remained holding the tablecloth as Norman took the microphone to introduce the act.

Norman walked across the stage, already getting the crowd into a frenzy.

"How are we all feeling tonight?"

Dropping the mic, bending forward at the waist, placing his hand to his ear, he goaded the audience to scream and shout, continuing encouragement into second and third waves of vocal mayhem.

"Are you having a good time?" He repeated the routine sending the audience into hysterics before taking control of the room again. "As some of you might know, I'm Norman Gosney...."

Girls started to hoot and he raised one eyebrow in a cheeky grin, pointing to a few of them in the audience. They were officially wound up, so he decided to get on with it.

"Now, you lucky people! Here tonight, right now, right here, you are about to witness history in the making folks. That's right folks, right here on the illuminated runway of joy, I'm proud to bring you just an example, just a tease, of the kind of entertainment we will be bringing to you nightly at China's first and only burlesque and vaudeville nightclub, Gosney and Kallman's Chinatown!"

The audience cheered.

"It's my honor. No, it's my privilege, to bring to you, straight from the stages of New York City, the one, the only, and tonight, Shanghai's very own, in 'The Bride of Frankenstein', ladies and gentlemen, put your hands together for Miss ...A...melia!"

Norman left the stage with a flourish, Dougie removed the curtain. Time stood still. The audience gasped. For a moment I was scared that there was a problem with the CD, but then the dark instrumental music proclaimed itself in a thundering roar. As The Bride, I was woken up by Dr. Frankenstein after several attempts. My initial hysterics are calmed by the doctor, who eventually seduces me into lying down with him where he removes my gown, causing me to jump up, intrigued by my own body in my underwear. Then I invite him to touch me and after some mimed banter he pokes each breast, then starts rubbing them manically until I slap his wrist, scolding him. He walks his fingers down my stomach, on top of my white cotton undies, and grabs between my legs, sending me into ecstasy simultaneously with the climax of the music. Blackout. Silence.

Then uproarious clapping and hollering ensued. I took a deep, relieved breath. I'd done it! The lights came back on, I bowed and exited. It couldn't have gone better and I felt a rush of exhilaration as Dougie helped me off stage, covering me again with the tablecloth. The audience carried on their approval for some time, bellowing through the venue, reaching out onto the street.

Star and Kayla were waiting for me in the bathroom.

"Oh my god, you were so good! I loved it. I want to do that," Kayla said hugging me.

"You are very good. I never see dance like that. Very good," said Star.

"Babe!" Dougie came bursting into the ladies room and stuffed my head to his chest in a suffocating bear hug. "That was so freakin' awesome! I'm so proud that I get to work with you guys. You freakin' rocked it babe."

Norman was already back out on the floor taking full advantage of the hype, whispering to the right people, 'Did you like that? Then invest in our nightclub. This is the coming brand... Someone's going to make a fortune off of this here in Asia, and I intend to be the first. You want in?'

I was coming out of a trance. When I'm on stage there isn't a part of me that's not one hundred percent present and invested in that moment. It gets me so high that it's hard to come back down to reality. I was pleased with myself that I had the guts to just go for it, insisting that Norman let me put up a burlesque.

Dougie helped me get the puppet unattached from my body before kissing me on the forehead and excusing himself to give me some privacy. It's always in those first few seconds of being alone after a performance that I feel the most aware of myself. It pleases my soul to be onstage. It's a gift and I love to give it.

First stop, the bar. I got mobbed by a gang offering me their congratulations, asking if they could buy me a drink. Well if you insist, a Tanqueray martini, straight up, shaken, with a twist. Time to get this party started! While I waited, a couple of camp gays and drunk girls I didn't know fawned over me.

"I totally, like, thought that he was real. Like, for real," one of the cute Brazilian boys said to me. "He looked like a midget and I was thinking, 'How did she get a midget on her shoulder? Is she carrying him?' and then he told me it was a puppet and I was like, 'No!' I couldn't believe it. Oh my god it was so good. And your body - Girl! I loved it and I love you."

Thank you darling.

Martini in hand, the band began their second set and I graciously excused myself to go watch our man, Freddy, in action.

A hand grabbed my arm and I turned around defensively to see a woman in a black flapper dress, drink in hand, and a tiny top hat pinned into her blonde hair.

"Hi! You're Amelia right? I'm Heidi-Sue. Everyone's been saying that I have to meet you."

I smiled automatically with my eyes attaching to her distracting cheek piercing that looked like a semi-precious pimple. She saddled up next to me like an old friend. I wondered if I should remember her from somewhere.

"Are you American?" I asked.

"Yeah, I'm from Utah."

"I'm American too. From right outside D.C in Virginia. Then New York."

She was the first other American I'd met in Shanghai. People are always surprised when I say that's where I'm from, remarking that most Americans don't travel abroad. Then it's practically a requirement to remark that I didn't vote for George W. Bush in order to avoid social rejection. He's done terrible things for America's international reputation, something I wouldn't have even been aware of in the States. I also get a lot of, 'But you're not fat', or 'You're pretty smart for an American'. Ouch.

"How's Utah? I've never been." I wondered what kind of American she was. Not a fat one, I could see that.

"Utah's great! Lots of Burners. I'm kind of a Burner myself. You know, Burning Man? Lots of Mormons in Salt Lake too. My family's all Mormon. My uncle's running for president."

"How about that." I took a sip of my martini, not sure how to respond.

"I used to do a lot of that kind of performance. Except of course, I'm not afraid to get my tits out," she giggled.

"Excuse me?"

"I am so glad someone is finally doing it here, I miss it so much. I also do stilts and fire, and I'm a fashion designer, and I can do some really amazing costumes." If she wanted me to be impressed, I wasn't.

"So do you think you could introduce me to Norman? I'd like to talk to him about his club."

"Well, actually, I'm probably the one to talk to. I'm the director of the show. We own the club together. He's my husband. But yeah, I'll give you my card. Send me an email next week and we can set something up."

I could tell she had her eye on being a showgirl, but I wasn't sure she was right. She was a bit older than the other girls, and not quite as attractive. There was something manly about her. Her comment about me not going down to nipple tassels, as if it was something I should be ashamed of, didn't exactly win me over either, but I liked the sound of her skills and slipped her business card into my cleavage.

Freddy called my name from the stage and I pardoned myself, rushing into his view. He called for another round of applause in my honor and I raised my gloved hand and waved to the room like Miss America. I spotted Norman and headed over to him as Freddy launched into 'That's Life'. Norm was standing with a short, white, round-faced man, whose uneven features instantly reminded me of an animated rat from a Disney movie. He was wearing a Burberry scarf and speaking intensely. I didn't want to interrupt as it looked important, but Norman saw me and took my hand to kiss it.

"And this is my lovely wife, Miss Amelia. Amelia, this is Remco Bredenberg." The man shook my hand and we kissed on both cheeks.

"I loved your performance," he said with a Swedish accent, "You are smarter than most women I know."

He laughed, as if that was supposed to be funny, but I let it slide and thanked him. He continued speaking to Norman. Freddy sang a few more songs, finishing with 'Black Magic', and then doing 'New York, New York' as an encore. Local and expat girls danced on banquets. The whole first floor waved their drinks in the air, singing along at the top of their lungs in drunken revelry. Kayla and Star joined me on either side looking over the balcony. They were both in love with their new roles as sparkling, glamazon showgirls.

I gave them each a kiss on the cheek as Kayla said, "We're going to rule this city! I can't wait."

We squealed a bit as girls do, before shouting out the end of 'New York, New York' along with everyone else, fists and drinks in the air. *If I can make it there, I'll make it anywhere!*

After it was over, people started to disperse. I found Dougie and Norman having a quiet huddle under the stairs.

"Darling," Norman said, "Great job tonight, I'm so proud of you. You nailed it. So baby, that guy I just introduced you to, Remco. He is serious money, and connections. He just happened to be here tonight because he's a friend of Len's and a jazz fan and he's… seriously interested in investing. Plus he asked all the right questions, so he's not a complete dick."

"But he's not Chinese," I said.

"No, but he has plenty of guangxi, just the kind we need too. I'll tell you more about it later. So, what are you up for then?" he continued. "Do you want to go out and party with the girls at the Sewer? Because I need to stick around and pursue Remco here while he's hot. But you and Dougie should go out and enjoy yourselves, you've earned it. Is that okay with you lover?"

I kissed him good-bye. Dougie and I followed our friends around the corner to a dance club called Shelter, built in an old fallout shelter of tunnels and caverns. We refer to it as 'The Sewer' because of its permanent rank smell.

Heidi-Sue was there. She made a point to dance provocatively in my sightline and flirt with Dougie, which caused a fight between her and a tall black guy, who stormed off. She stayed and drank more, flashing her bum and panties as she danced. Maybe she would make a good showgirl.

I was starting to feel pretty drunk, so I leaned over and told Dougie I was going home.

"Do you want me to come too? Will you be okay?" he shouted over the drum and bass.

I assured him I'd be fine and picked up my Chinese laundry bag with Dr. Frankenstein tucked away inside, and motioned for him to follow me into the slightly quieter hallway tunnel.

"You sure you're okay to get home?" he said again, slurring his words.

It was a sweet sentiment, but a dumb question. We both knew very well there would be twenty cabs lined up outside, and we only lived three blocks away.

"I'll be fine," I said reaching up to give him a hug.

He lifted me off the ground, and when he put me back down he looked into my eyes.

"I just want you to know," he said, "and don't take this the wrong way or anything, but I just want you to know, I'll always be here for you."

I smiled thinking he was done, but he continued.

"If anything, I mean anything, if anything happens to Norman or anything, don't worry, I'll take care of you, I promise."

He kissed me on the forehead for a long second, before turning around and rushing off into the blackness. I walked up the stairs to the street, and told the cab driver where to go before replaying his last sentence in my head. It struck me as odd, but then again, we were both pretty drunk.

Dougie didn't come home until two days later. His phone was going straight to voicemail, which concerned us after awhile, especially because it brought up issues of what to do if something happened to one of us. How would we even know where to start? Call the hospitals or police stations where no one spoke English? I knocked on the door to his room before peeking in and turning on the light, just to make sure he wasn't lying dead in his own vomit or something. There was a stench from an open can of spoiling sardines with two forks sticking out of it and a used condom knotted on the unmade bed. I quickly shut the door again, wishing I hadn't seen that.

When Dougie finally did turn up he was a disheveled, confused mess. Norman took him aside for a man-to-man chat. He relayed to me later that, after I had left The Sewer, Dougie had gotten very drunk, brought two hookers back to our house and fucked them before they 'kidnapped' him, took him to an ATM, made him take out a couple grand and brought him to a hotel. He didn't know what day it was, how long he'd been out for, where his cellphone was, whether or not he had lost his new laptop. In short, he was a wreck.

I was disgusted with him mostly because he brought prostitutes into my house. I had to go around checking to make sure all our stuff was still there since they're known for stealing whatever they can get their hands on. Norman also told me that Dougie confided that he is bi-polar and the medicine he takes regularly for it can have bad side effects when mixed with alcohol and stops him from getting a hard-on. So that night he had taken some Viagra on top of the drinks and other drugs, which apparently wasn't a good idea. I accepted his apology and gave him my forgiveness when he asked for it. But I wasn't happy.

It reminded me of the day we became business partners and my horoscope had warned that relationships made at that time would disappoint me a year down the line. I'm not one to take horoscopes to heart, but for some reason, this one stuck with me.

CHAPTER 15 – Feng Shui, Fuck Shui

The guys scoped him out. Remco Bredenberg was who he claimed to be. He had lived in China over twenty years, spoke fluent Mandarin, Cantonese, Shanghainese and seven other dialects. He owned a multinational interior design company. Ten years ago he got a lot of attention when he sued a local supplier that severely ripped him off. He threatened to go public to the rest of the world, telling businesses not to come to China, that it was backwards and corrupt. At the time it was a big enough threat that he won the high-profile case, making him the first - and one of only a few - expats to ever win a court case against a Chinese company.

Norman, Dougie and I went to Remco's sprawling headquarters out West, beyond Gubei. His impressive office was covered with photos of himself glad-handing Chinese officials, celebrities and bigwigs. He showed no Western-style qualms when bragging about or exhibiting his guangxi.

"You know," Remco said to us in an obscure cross between a Swedish and Chinese accent, "I've been here a long time. I'm married to a local girl whose family is connected and I've still gotten screwed over by the Chinese more times than I'd like to admit. More times than I've had success, I will say that. Your project, Chinatown, has never been done in this country before. On paper, it can't be done. It's impossible. You'll get a lot of attention, you'll get jealousy, you'll get harassment and you'll get problems. But it's not impossible. Not if you are partners with someone like me. You need someone with a lot of guangxi and I am a person who can provide that. I wouldn't commit to a project if I didn't believe in the potential for it to be a success. I see you both and what you did the other night and I believe in you. I see your passion and determination, and I want to help you."

He spoke frankly, which we appreciated. I can't say that I exactly liked Remco. He was more Chinese than any Swede I'd ever known. We'd heard so many stories about the dangers of having a local partner though, and here was a guy, a surrogate Chinese but nominally European, who had the necessary guangxi. In any other country, under any other circumstances, Remco would've been too straight, too materialistic, too much of a nerd for us to want to get into bed with. I had to wonder if all the photos and branded clothes were part of a front to please the Chinese, or if he had been there so long that he'd traded in his culture for theirs. A hard call. While this guy didn't have a cool bone in his body, he had an exceptional understanding of the ins and outs of doing business in China, which was something we very much needed.

He agreed to buy a block of shares in the company, investing half the money then and the other half when the remaining investment needed to open came in from a third, still unknown party. Norman and I had already invested in securing the premises, but Remco's investment would be enough to move forward with construction on the site. Remco assigned us one of his employees, Goldfish, to work full-time on the task of getting us legal and open. Her responsibilities included dealing with the massive amounts of paperwork needed to secure our licensing, and most importantly, being our liaison to the Cultural Department. She would also keep us abreast of all the appropriate, requested and required bribes. With black-rimmed- glasses, Goldfish dressed like a dowdy, cakey librarian. And I don't think she brushed her teeth.

Goldfish had us buy a three thousand-kwai Louis Vuitton wallet as a bribe to give Mr. Lao, the landlord's man-on-site, as we were asking to have more electrical power usage from the building's supply. We had to wrap the wallet with the receipt enclosed so Mr. Lao could see it was the real, expensive, name brand item, bought from the store, as opposed to a knock-off. In contrast, it had to be given in a brown paper bag since it couldn't be seen to be a bribe. Because of course, we all know, 'There is no bribery in China'.

Goldfish discovered a sentence in the labyrinthine regulations saying that there could be no entertainment or alcohol served in a heritage building, such as ours – a potentially devastating discovery this late in the game. The given reason? It might conjure up dead spirits. Having dealt with New York's squeaky tight club regulations, a million bye-laws that cover everything from proximity to churches, to over-zealous wheelchair access, Norman thought he'd heard it all... But this one took the rice cake.

Prior to the Japanese invasion of China in 1937, our building had been the cultural center for the large Nippon community in Shanghai. Like the Jews, the Japanese deal with their dead as quickly as possible. Soldiers who perished in Shanghai were cremated immediately and their urns stored in our future premises. The intention had been to ship the urns back to the appropriate homeland shrine when the war was over, but when the Japanese were defeated, they slipped out of Shanghai in the middle of the night, leaving everything behind, including the ashes. The Chinese ransacked the former temple, threw all the ashes into the streets and pissed on them. No wonder there was concern about angry spirits from the past.

Demonstrating his immense guangxi, Remco pulled off nothing short of a miracle and got us a last minute meeting on a Friday afternoon in front of all the most powerful men in Shanghai: The Governor of Hongkou, the Head of Commerce and Foreign Investment, the Head of Culture, and the Head of Parks and Recreation. The meeting was to convince them to make an exception on the no alcohol and entertainment policy for our heritage building. The meeting opened with Goldfish handing out brown paper bags to all the men, each containing stacks of hundred kwai notes. Norman explained the project to them in terms they could grasp, describing it again as 'A Broadway show in a 1930's theme bar'.

After Norman's spiel, the officials and Remco spoke at length in their local dialect, cutting us foreigners out of the conversation completely. Many cigarettes later, we got a response: An across the board pledge of support for Chinatown! No minor feat. If any one of those guys had said no, which they were in complete authority to do, the project would've been shut down instantly. They had their own interests in getting expat business into the Hongkou district in time for the 2010 World Expo. Remco had successfully convinced them that Chinatown was a good thing for everyone. Victory was ours! Now we could finally move ahead.

Norman jumped straight onto on the task of finding the right contractor to do the construction on the club. Again, there had been quite a few warnings about disastrous local crook contractors from friends. Expats who had been in China awhile never hesitated to bitch and moan about the endless nightmares of the constant corruption one faces when doing business, especially in construction. Norman set up interviews with half a dozen recommended companies, including a company that Remco had recently used to do one of his showrooms. In New York, Norman ran a small construction company to fit out his venues, and had the experience to know all the most important issues one must address when building a nightclub. Things like sound proofing, acoustics, Feng Shui, Fuck Shui. He had it all down to a science.

He began weeding out the slimy, double-talking contractors from the ones slightly less slimy and double-talking. In the end he chose Harley Zhou and his construction team, the one Remco had recommended. Harley claimed he didn't understand English well, but you could tell he was listening closely. Average height, he had a wide, muscular build, but his shoulders sloped down at ninety-degree angles.

Harley always had a cigarette in one hand, a cell phone in the other, and a perturbed look about him. He had an abnormally large head, puffy cheeks, and a mole on his chin with a single, two-inch long hair coming out of it. Mole hair is considered lucky in China, the longer the luckier. Go figure.

Norman chose Harley's company over the others because he contemplated and answered questions thoughtfully and, for the most part, came up with the right answers. He was also the only one to include an estimate upfront of how much the job would cost in bribes. Harley knew a lot of people too and claimed to have the guangxi in the Hongkou district to cut bargain deals. The amounts that would go to factions of the government, like the fire department and the gas and electric companies, were substantial. After consulting with Magic, who said these figures weren't exaggerated, explaining it as, 'The price of doing business in China', Norman took this as a sign of attempted honesty and transparency, a rare and precious commodity in China. A deal was made.

After a Buddhist cleansing ceremony to remove any lingering ghosts, ground was broke at last. Over twenty workers moved on site, living, working, eating and sleeping there around the clock. The first thing they did was tear everything back to the dirt, leaving only the original walls, the bar, stairs, the original arched framework and the foundation of what would become the second floor balcony.

Walking in, I immediately felt light headed from the dust, toxic fumes and cigarette smoke in our unventilated, windowless building. Norman gave me a mask to wear. It was hard to believe that none of the workers wore masks or safety gear. A couple of buff, hardened, weathered women worked tirelessly, doing backbreaking, repetitive labor right alongside the men. Two school-aged children and a toddler also lived on site, running around, left to amuse themselves. The only light came from one electrical wire with bulbs every ten feet, strung in the same fashion that I had been warned against in fourth grade science class. A definite fire hazard. Norman commented on it, baffled, but sort of threw his hands in the air, saying that there was no use arguing with 'The Chinese way'. At great expense, we would have to put in entirely new electrics throughout the whole building and even draw major new power in from a block away.

We climbed over mounds of bamboo ready to be assembled into scaffolding, to where the kitchen would be. At the moment it was just a bare room with a dirt floor and some holes in the walls. It was set up like a shantytown for the workers with wood slabs laid over cement bricks for beds, well worn *Toy Story* blankets on top. In the center was a small camping stove with a big pot of white rice on it. Several of the men who were on their eight hour break before returning to another sixteen hour shift, crouched around it seated on paint cans, shoveling rice and cabbage into their mouths with chopsticks. I made a point to smile and tell them in Chinese that they were doing a great job. Norman grabbed me playfully by the waist and gave me a big wet kiss, pointing to my wedding ring, then to himself, smiling absurdly for the men. The guys grinned and nodded.

Then I pointed to Norman and said, "Ta Fengle!" and they spat out their food laughing. They invited me to come sit with them and offered me some of their food. I'd won them over.

"What'd you say?" Norman whispered as we continued our tour.

"Nothing... just that you are crazy... I think they agree."

Norman showed me where the bathrooms would go. Unbelievably, there had never been a plumbing system in the building, not even when it had been a snooker parlor or a KTV, so we would have to build from the sewage system up to get toilets into the building, another considerable cost. On the second floor he showed me a major leak, which meant putting a whole new roof on the building. Then there was an AC to be installed as well. He pointed out where the adjacent building encroached on our territory, taking a chunk out of our real estate for their own use. The area had been given to the building behind ours as a settlement for a dispute between the cheap hotel and the low-end brothel that share the same building. The workers who used the hotel didn't want to be seen coming and going from the same entrance the brothel used, so the solution had been to thieve a bit of our property. We were still paying for the square footage though, of course.

"A brothel? Right there? But didn't we have to sign all kinds of papers promising that we weren't going to run a brothel or have hookers working here? Didn't they make a really big deal about it, saying that they'd shut us down and we'd go to jail?"

"Yup!" he said, too exasperated with the double standard to try explaining it. "Maybe they don't want the competition. One rule for them, one rule for us. That's how it is." He sighed. "Come with me."

He took me outside and around to our neighboring building, the entrance meant for the people staying at the hotel. On the landing under flickering fluorescent lights, there was a wall-sized poster of a beach with palm trees, sun and sand that read 'Welcome to Paradise Hotel'. Paradise was a far cry from the reality of the closet-sized rooms with the single, short beds they offered. I followed Norman out a window onto a roof where clothes hung drying in the breeze. We climbed up a precarious ladder to the roof of our building. Standing on top, the scene I took in made me feel nauseated. Norman stood there in the corner next to me and didn't need to say a thing.

"Oh my god," I whispered for lack of better words.

Our barreled roof had a drainage gulley around it, now piled ten feet high in garbage. Literally. Some of it was bagged, but mostly it was just loose rubbish, like a city dump. Old bicycle pieces, dirty baby diapers, sickened carpets, paint cans, broken toys and reeking trash bags, thick with flies. The rancid, rotting stench wafted in our direction. It was the weight from this trash that had caused the leak in our roof.

Peering up at the apartment building that looked down onto the stinking heap, I momentarily felt bad for the people who have to live next to this atrocity. A pug-faced, chubby teenager leaned out one of the windows. He stared at us for a second. Then I realized: It was these motherfuckers throwing the rubbish out their windows onto the roof! The guy disappeared.

"You know, we have to give a huge bribe to the sanitation department," Norman said. "And have to build an annex on the side of our building to keep our trash locked up in. All part of their rules. Just over there are three industrial sized rubbish bins for these apartments, but why bring your trash downstairs when you can just throw it out your window onto your neighbor's roof?"

As he said that, the teenager returned to his window and threw a paper bag of food trash down at us, aiming for our heads, cigarette hanging from his mouth, daring us to react.

"What the fuck?" Norman shouted, looking up, "You nasty man."

The guy left the window. We decided not to wait around to find out what he was going to throw next.

When we got out to the courtyard, Norm introduced me to his new friend the shoe repairman, who sat outside our building at his portable workshop. The spiky-hair man looked at me funny when I shook his blackened hand and said in my best Mandarin, 'Hěn gāoxìng rènshì nǐ', or nice to meet you. He gave me a faint shake, but wouldn't look at me directly.

This was really starting to frustrate me. I'd been trying so hard to learn and speak Mandarin, but most of the time my attempts to communicate were met with a lack of willingness to respond. Winnie, my tutor, assured me that I was getting the difficult inflections correct, so why wasn't anyone talking back to me? I couldn't tell whether to take it as rudeness or insecurity, arrogance or surprise, or what.

Even though it tested my patience, I was determined not to lose hope. Being accepted by the Chinese and having local friends was important to me, and speaking Mandarin was one way to show that I respect and like their culture. Shanghai has a reputation for being an unfriendly, tough city to penetrate, similar to New York or London in that way, but we were in it for the long haul. China was my home for the foreseeable future, and while I was fully committed to my new life, I missed feeling like an accepted member of the community. I longed for that. That's why I knew that if I wanted to fit in, I couldn't give up. Ignore me all you want, but I wasn't going to stop trying.

CHAPTER 16 – Joining a Cult

A middle-aged, tubby, balding, French drag queen, Luc René, a.k.a. Lady Saturn, came on board to assist in choreographing our production numbers. He claimed to be the only performing drag queen in China. Homosexuality became legal in China in 1997, and taken off the mental illness list in 2001. Shanghai, the most liberal of the cities in the People's Republic, had an active gay scene with whole sections of expat magazines devoted to it. But raids on gay clubs still happened every couple of months. Like so many things in the city that appeared permissible, it was at the mercy of someone's whim. Tomorrow they could decide to put all the homosexuals in jail if they wanted to and no one could do a thing about it. I quite like gay men and get along with them well, but Luc René was everything a paunchy, over-the-hill, hair-challenged, French drag queen promised to be: Namely, a bitch. But his choreography was what I asked for, he taught it well, and he was what the city had to offer.

Irene was fired not long into rehearsals because she refused to smile, and that is one requirement of being a showgirl. Making her stay after rehearsal, I asked her to prove to me that she could in fact dance and smile at the same time, but she couldn't, so she was out. Shortly after that, her friend Natasha stopped showing up for rehearsals too. That's when I decided to hire Josephine the pole dancer, and Heidi-Sue the Mormon.

The Chinatown Dolls were rehearsing our signature opening number, 'Six Terrific Girls (But Only Five Costumes)'. The emcee sings the song and introduces each showgirl individually center stage, as they each remove the thick pink taffeta boas to reveal rose-covered bras and knickers, complimented by wide brim, southern-belle hats and thigh-high white, gartered stockings. All the girls that is, except for Kayla, who comes in from the audience as if running late, smoking a joint and wearing a long, white-shag coat and a hip-length blonde wig. She jumps onstage, disrobes and takes her position on a riser in the back center. Her virtually naked body is semi- hidden behind the other showgirls until the reveal at the end when she comes forward in a diamond g-string, and sparkling pasties. Like the song says, '*Take six terrific girls, but only five costumes, and you've got a bur-lesque show*'.

From London we imported a former captain of the Welsh Guards named Rupert Loughery, to be the club's emcee. Norman was retiring from his customary role in favor of a larger one, hosting the room. We knew Rupert because he used to come to our speakeasy in New York with Alan Cumming, and was a fan of our work. We saw him host several events and fashion shows, and were attracted to how he worked a crowd with his British command tone. Rupert stood six-foot-three and rail thin, with dark brown hair and seductive eyes, he resembled Ralph Fiennes. His cross between child-like openness and military manliness made him quite unpredictable, but at the same time irresistible to both women and men alike. It was hard to tell whose attentions he preferred more.

I wrote him an email several months back inviting him to Shanghai to live in a company paid-for apartment and star in our show. When I didn't hear back from him I assumed he wasn't interested. I thought it was strange though that I didn't get any reply. Then one day out of the blue, I got an email. He apologized for not being in touch sooner. He'd been detained... at Her Majesty's Pleasure. That's Brit for 'in prison', Norman explained. But now that he was a free man again he would be thrilled to come work for us if the offer still stood. For some reason, having a criminal record actually made it clear to me that he was indeed the man for the job.

We rented an apartment just over Suzhou Creek near the club for Rupert, Dougie and Freddy. Being a trained actor, Rupert was apprehensive about being on stage without a script, so I gave him an alter ego, directing him to pretend he was a superhero, the mascot of the club. This gave him the permission he needed to be free from the fear of failing. And he was off.

We earned our first paycheck as a company hosting the Google Christmas party. Ironically, it was the week before Google pulled out of China. They alleged it was over censorship, but everyone knew it was because their systems were endlessly being hacked and their intelligence copied by the Chinese. The showgirls had pictures taken with the local employees one by one, and then we had to deliver the printed photo to them later in the evening. It sounds easy, right? But I swear, every man at that party wore a plain black suit, white shirt, red tie, glasses, had their black hair parted on the side, and were all Han Chinese. Recognizing who was who was like a live game of *Where's Waldo*.

Once word spread that the Chinatown crew was available for gigs, all kinds of parties started rolling in, including one of the oddest jobs we've ever done. We were hired by a wealthy expat industrialist to provide entertainment at a 'cult' themed party. Not an obvious theme for Shanghai, but a bold and intriguing one, nonetheless. We were instructed to go wild. We decided to make a deity the size of a child and named the androgynous holy prophet 'Devon'.

In the area around People's Square there were street after street of hair and wig supply stores where I hoped to find a mannequin head to be Devon's face. At the second store I went to there was a box next to the door containing discounted dummy heads. One in particular caught my eye. When I pulled it out for closer inspection, there was no question - I'd found Devon. It must've been a fuck up at the factory. I don't know how else you could explain it. Slightly cone-shaped, it had a life-like child's face on the front and on the back of the head, a second face, but that one was asleep. Super creepy! I debated whether or not it was too creepy. We made Devon a small body, dressing him in a velour jumpsuit with a Rolex, gold chains and a pair of Chanel sunglasses.

At the party he sat in a chair, unreachable on a small balcony, dimly lit and way mysterious behind layers of mesh curtains. People were invited to come into a candle lit room individually and ask him a deep, spiritual question. Norman hid under the table with a fixed tube running to the doll's mouth. He answered the questions as Devon in a Yorkshire accent. We copped The Church of the Sub-Genius propaganda off the internet to distribute at the party, infusing it with pictures of Devon and the party's date. We dressed in black from head to toe, with Afro wigs, headbands and sunglasses. Norman led a series of call-and-responses ending with us proclaiming robotically, 'Fuck them if they can't take a joke'.

We had Chinese girls take one look at him and run away screaming. Grown men burst into tears with quasi-spiritual, intoxicated awakenings. Devon instructed a guy and a girl to take off all their clothes and return to the party naked... And they did! It was unreal. Towards the end of the night, after Devon's room briefly and mysteriously caught fire, we carried him through the crowd of revelers, letting his hood slip off at just the right moment, revealing his second face. Even those who were in on it winced and jumped. Devon became an instant Shanghai legend.

Our first full-on, proper Chinatown production came on December 31st 2008, the foreigner's New Year's Eve. We did a show at a restaurant on the Bund exclusively for a hundred people. The Chinatown Dolls performed three production numbers, Kayla and Freddy sang a few songs, Norman and Rupert co-hosted together and Josephine performed a burlesque routine I directed. No one seemed to mind when one of her pasties popped off at the end of her act as she gave it some extra gusto on all fours on a table. The back wall of the restaurant, across from the performance area, had floor to ceiling windows without curtains, something that no one had considered. Halfway through the night Norman instructed the audience to turn around and look. Outside on the street there was a crowd of local faces two blocks deep. Maybe four hundred people were out there, cheering and waving at us. It reminded me New Year's Eve in Times Square.

CHAPTER 17 – The Great Leap Forward

Chinese New Year is a time traditionally spent with family. For the migrant workers it is the one-week off they have the entire year, making it the most important holiday in China. Nearly 180 million people are thought to travel during this time. All the factory workers take the money they've earned, board trains and buses with presents of oranges and red envelopes filled with cash, and travel back to visit their family in the villages of their origin.

In the lead up to this holiday in 2008, China experienced its heaviest snowstorm in fifty years. They weren't prepared in so many ways. Roads and train tracks were blocked, icy conditions proved hazardous, people froze to death. Tension between travelers and the military heightened. Chaos verging on an uprising. Passengers were asked to abandon their travel plans, which only enraged them more. The average Chinese guest worker toiling for peanuts in the booming cities will put up with many indignities and great hardships, but the Chinese New Years return to their families is an unfuckable-with right, never to be denied or trifled with.

That weekend it was estimated that six million people were left stranded at the stations, standing in the snow for days in tight crowds like sardines, without food, water or bathroom facilities, while they waited for the soldiers to finish shoveling the tracks. The military kept armed watch from looming tanks as people refused to accept that they might miss their precious few days of freedom. Cars sat in gridlock, several hundred people died, roofs collapsed and whole cities went without electricity, heat or water for over two weeks.

Gage told us that Mao had once made the arbitrary decision that everywhere below the Yangtze river didn't get cold enough to warrant heating, so he had all the central heating below the river line removed, regardless of the true weather. That included Shanghai, which, trust me, needs all the heat it can get come winter.

It was almost time for the guests of our Chinese New Year party to arrive. 2009: Year of the Ox. Last year was the Year of the Rat and Ikea sold whole matched sets of crockery covered in rats to celebrate.

One of Norman's best friends, Howie Costello, was visiting us from LA for a few weeks. Howie and Norman were sat at the table in front of a laptop when I came into the kitchen. Howie was showing Norman pictures of his new, secret, pornstar girlfriend on a website sticking soda cans up her pussy. Yup. Howie was in town. Norman was flabbergasted by him already and looked at me bewildered before asking if they could please talk about something else now that I was in the room.

Presents! He brought us presents from the States. For Norman, a stack of New Yorker magazines, and for me, three boxes of assorted absorbency Tampax tampons, which I requested since they don't do tampons in China. Yeah, you heard me.

Howie Costello was in his late forties and had a gold front tooth that used to have a diamond in it before he swallowed it. He had a full head of Italian black, rockabilly waxed hair and was ruggedly handsome in a greaser, throwback kind of way. He looked older than Norman though, from boozing and smoking and years of hunching over his equipment. A girl who wanted him off her back 'gave' Howie to Norman years ago. The two guys hit it off over their mutual love of jazz and Jamaican music, pleased to find a mate who knew complementary trivia. This resulted in epic conversations about the Top Ten Greatest this or that, the Most Influential, the Unsung Heroes, etc. They soon considered each other brothers.

We were enjoying showing off our city to Howie, taking him on bicycle tours all over town. Being able to show one of our old mates around Shanghai reminded us again of all the things we loved about the city: The beauty of the quiet, tree-lined streets of the French Concession at night, the long lanes, or 'longshans', the neighborhoods where real China street life remained virtually frozen in time; The waltzers in the park, the cheap and delicious street food, the ability to easily make the locals smile and laugh. Despite the challenges, Shanghai was still one of the greatest cities in the world, and as the pace of change continued steadily, having Howie around gave us an opportunity to slow down and really appreciate the time and place we were living in.

Norman says Howie is a near genius when it comes to music, but he's a near disaster when it comes to women. Always the wrong one, the wrong approach, just wrong. He once got dropped off on Norman's doorstep at the Chelsea Hotel by a famous actor who Howie refers to behind his back as 'Garbage Dick' or GD for short. GD said that Howie had gone off his meds again and was out of his mind over another wrong woman. He wouldn't stop talking, wasn't eating or making sense. GD and Norman tried to do what they could. After several fraught episodes involving the hotel staff, hospitals and other shenanigans, Howie eventually snapped out of it, but refused to ever speak about the episode. He'd been better these last few years, besides some indications of depression and several weirdo girlfriends who came and went.

The doorbell rang. Our first party guest, Winnie, my tutor, arriving twenty minutes early.

"Xīn Nián Kuài Lè!" we both exclaimed as she handed me a carton of orange juice.

I hadn't expected her to come honestly, I assumed she would be with her family. We sat together in my living room uncomfortably trying to come up with things to talk about. Then Star arrived early too, much to my relief. She came trotting in loaded for bear, afraid that us foreigners wouldn't have the right supplies for a proper Chinese New Year party.

Star looked like a modern calendar girl in a short, metallic red, traditional qípáo dress. She bustled into the kitchen with a grocery bag full of goodies and put it down on the table before turning to tell me the rules.

"Okay," she said looking me up and down. I couldn't remember ever seeing her so serious. "You are dressed... umm... okay, you have red, but today you no wear black and no wear white because you get bad luck."

She said this with conviction, as if she was sincerely worried for my well being in my black leggings and tight white t-shirt with red sequins lips on it.

"Okay," she said again, which was a new verbal tick of hers, one that I'm afraid she may have picked up from me. "You can no wash hair for three days and no say number..." she held up four fingers, "but six and eight have good luck and are good to say."

"Six and eight!" I played along.

"And you have to buy new pants for good luck, but no shoes. And do not break things or do sweeping." She waved a disciplinary finger in my direction.

Star unloaded her groceries, handing me red and gold streamers, stacks of firecrackers, and white, gelatinous, fish-shaped sweets that she warned not to eat a whole one because that would be like eating all my luck and then I'd have none leftover. As we set up a dumpling assembly line, the doorbell kept ringing. Heidi-Sue showed up early to help out and brought homemade brownies. She arrived with a tall, attractive Cameroonian guy named Nez, who I embarrassingly mistook to be her husband. She laughed it off though and explained she'd left him at home to look after her son. When I asked how they met the two just giggled. Heidi-Sue told me that Nez could sing in Mandarin, an act I said I'd like to see sometime.

Soon the house was filled with people. Norman and Howie were spinning the tunes, and every room had people drinking, laughing, dancing, and eating. When Norman introduced Heidi-Sue to Howie, I watched her adding him to a mental list of guys she wanted to fuck. Putting him above Nez, it appeared.

Then Dougie arrived with the guest of honor. He had started to court wealthy, middle-aged women he met in bars. He would tell them about Chinatown, minimize our need for investment and hang himself out as a carrot to take one for the team. A Chinese millionaire divorcee who drove a red convertible and always wore expensive, unmatched outfits, started paying him to sleep with her. She set him up in his own apartment before telling him she had no intention of investing in the club. She wanted him to be her full-time boy-toy.

Then Dougie met Beth Peterson. A fellow Aussie, she was the Chief Event Coordinator for the city's top event firm. She had contacted him about hiring The Chinatown Dolls for an upcoming corporate gig. The two hit it off as drinking buddies, but Dougie didn't think anymore of it until she happened to mention that she had received a large inheritance and was looking into investments. He gave her the soft sell. When he realized she was serious, up to the tune of a block of shares that would be sufficient enough to get us open, he may have given her the impression that if she invested they could be more than just business partners. She wanted to meet us first though, so Dougie suggested she accompany him to our party.

About five-foot-four, Beth had long blonde hair down to her waist and fragile, pale blue eyes. She had a pointy nose and small lips. I hadn't expected her to be so attractive in the face - she was beautiful - or so large in the body. I don't mean that in a mean way, it's just not everyday you see a bigger person in these parts, it stands out. She wore all black and had a bottle of vodka in each hand.

"Xīn Nián Kuài Lè!" Dougie shouted making his grand entrance. Norman and I made a beeline to them.

"It's so good to finally meet you! Thank you so much for coming. You look gorgeous by the way," I greeted Beth warmly.

She looked down at herself, shrugging off the compliment. "Euh! I've had this old thing for years. But we brought vodka!"

I waited to see her smile, but she never really did. Maybe I only noticed because I'd just been chatting to Julie Helm, former Miss Hong Kong, who was lecturing me intently about how I smiled too much. She said that if I kept it up, by the time I was her age I'd be covered in wrinkles. She added that she gives the same advice to her five-year-old daughter. You know, because it's never too early to start not smiling.

"That's why Chinese women have such smooth skin and we are very mysterious. And you know if we smile we mean it," Julie told me. It's a good point, but I can't help it, I'm a smiler.

Norman was the one to get Beth to crack. He approached her formally, bowed, clicked his heels together, brought her hand to his mouth, inspecting her rings as if wearing a monocle, and kissed the back of her hand. He held her eyes until she had to bend her lips and blush. Dougie made introductions. Beth downed her first drink and started on a second. I introduced her to the showgirls and showboys who were pre-instructed to make her feel welcomed.

"Dougie tells me you're a singer," I said, trying to break the ice.

"Yeah, I sing." I waited for her to continue, but she just stared straight ahead, clutching her drink.

"Well, you'll have to sing at the club sometime. Dougie can play the drums, I'll play the guitar, and Norman can.... What can you do honey?"

"I can dance!" He stood up and broke into his best Mick Jagger, pointing, puffing out his lips and thrusting his pelvis wildly in the faces of Gage and the shy, petite local girl he'd brought as his date, making the room spill with laughter, and drinks.

Excusing myself to the bathroom, I walked into my bedroom where Rupert was on the bed sandwiched between a small, fay Filipino boy and a skinny, gamine British girl. They were lying in a sexy huddle, with Rupert blissfully in the center.

"Sorry," I said passing through, trying not to look.

"It's okay," said the Filipino boy. "Want to join?"

Three pairs of horny eyes and opened legs looked at me.

In New York we had a friend who used to run very high-end, exclusive sex parties out of Bob Dylan's old room at The Chelsea Hotel. It would be full of partially undressed, really good-looking people piled up on top of each other, humping and groaning, what we jokingly referred to as 'frogging'. Our burlesque girls strolled around serving drinks in nothing but pasties, garter belts, knickers and stockings. In one room there would be a woman getting gang-banged while her husband jerked off. In another, girls gave lap dances, while others had their tits painted in edible ink. They were the wildest, best parties in New York, and I always left feeling... enlightened.

Snapping back into reality, I kindly turned the hungry hedonists down. Those days of experimentation had been exhilarating, and while I think everyone needs to have at least one experience like that in their lives, seeing Rupert and his friends there reminded me that I was happy to be in a stable healthy, two-person relationship with someone I love and trust.

When I came out from the bathroom, Rupert was on top of both the guy and girl, kissing them simultaneously with one arm around the guy's neck and his other hand up the girl's skirt. The girl rubbed her stocking-legs together, and Rupert reached between them, while focusing his tongue down the boy's throat. Four hands reached for Rupert's cock. It looked like a hot mess. I shut the door behind me.

Back in the living room, a girl approached me.

"Hi! You're Amelia right?" She had long, straight auburn hair, light brown Cleopatra eyes, and freshly sun-kissed skin. She wore a loose purple, satin dress and cute black heels, showing off her slim, toned legs. "I'm Brenna," she said with an Aussie accent, "Rupert's friend."

"He's got a lot of friends, doesn't he?" I remarked with a smile before I could stop myself.

She wanted to talk about the club and the show and when we were going to open. Everyone wanted to know when we were going to open. That question was beginning to feel like a thorn in my side. Brenna told me that she'd been a dancer her whole life and would love to be a showgirl. She was pretty enough to be a showgirl and she had an aura of positive, peaceful energy around her. A good mix of feistiness and smarts. At this point, adding a new foxy girl to the chorus line could only benefit us, and maybe it would inspire a little healthy competition, upping everyone's game. At the very least, we could always use an understudy.

Star interrupted us to say goodbye. She was off to have dinner with her boyfriend's family. It would be her third dinner that evening. She complimented me on a successful Chinese New Year party, and I was touched when she proclaimed she was proud of me.

Returning to the kitchen, I joined a conversation with a friend who writes for the Wall Street Journal. He had recently snuck into Sichuan Province, posing as a bereaved family member. It was ten months since the earthquake occurred, but he relayed that there was no reconstruction being done on the disaster zone. The government had taped sections off in a football field, dividing it into minute strips where the survivors were confined to live for an indefinite period of time, receiving two bowls of rice a day. The army stood guard. Cellphones and internet service remained shutdown. He said he couldn't report on these things for fear it would put him and his family in danger. He had colleagues who had been deported, or imprisoned, for their reports on China.

The Olympics was another hot topic. We had to wonder how much of what we knew to be the truth was known by the rest of the world. It was common knowledge that the Chinese had spray-painted the grass green, and seeded the clouds so it wouldn't rain, but we wondered if anyone was able to get reports out about why the required area for protest remained conspicuously empty. The people who had applied for peaceful protest licenses were rounded up and imprisoned for the duration of the games. For several days during the Olympics the government cut off the entire country's internet service.

Another friend of mine, Simon, chimed in saying that he believed China was becoming more like North Korea everyday, but with money, resources and a good PR strategy. He should know. Simon was the only person allowed to bring groups of tourists into North Korea. It was a trip I always planned to go on, especially because he doesn't believe foreigners will be allowed in for much longer.

Kayla arrived at the party looking sensational in a silver, tight, backless mini-dress she made herself, accompanied by a young, hot, Parisian deejay, Claude, who had worked at the Paris opera and was part of a deejay duo called Acid Pony Club. He was interested in working tech at the club. I nodded for him to follow me and introduced him to Norman and Howie, and the three of them were immediately off, dropping names, talking tech and music.

We moved the party outside to the courtyard. The streets began to catch fire with flaming magic tricks. Fireworks and firecrackers sparkled and took flight, erupting in bursts. All our neighbors had their snakes of firecrackers going off like machine guns, making thick smoke and bellowing ash. Ballistic chaos erupted, driving the guys insane, giddy, possessed, cavemen playing with fire. Thrilling to watch. Also a little scary. Gage, who nominated himself the ringleader, explained that it's tradition to set crackers off in front of doorways to force out the bad spirits of last year and invite the new, good spirits in. He reminded us that we must be seen to do this in front of our club sometime that week.

The fire, smoke and explosive jangle transformed the streets into a jubilant warzone, a bombastic soundtrack to this unifying celebration. The boys took obscene pleasure in setting off bottle rockets behind the girl's backs, making us jump three feet in the air and cling to each other, screaming. That was just the beginning.

The big guns came out. Boxes of fireworks, launching rockets high into the air, bursting over our heads like rashes in the sky. They were the kind of boxes that have an entire pyrotechnic display in them, rockets, mortars, huge explosives. Just light the fuse and stand well back, mucho illegal in the States, as each one has the equivalent firepower of a bad night in Beirut. It was out of this world. Intense and exhilarating... and never-ending.

I noticed the neighborhood spy and even uniformed police officers getting in on the action, officially sanctioned anarchy. It was a free-for-all like nothing I could've possibly imagined. I stood in a huddle with Josephine, Kayla and Heidi-Sue, covering our ears, letting out squeals, and watching the sky fall to pieces above us.

"Don't you like it?" Gage said with a sinister grin, like the mask of Alan Moore's *V for Vendetta*.

"This is nuts!" I shouted over the noise.

"Well you better get used to it, it's going to be like this for the next ten days."

He wasn't kidding either. Us girls looked at each other, deciding to go back inside for more drinks and brownies.

The mayhem outside continued relentlessly through the night. A lot of people took this as a cue to get on their bikes, as the night was still young and there were more parties to attend. We started our own little dance party in the apartment. Rupert rejoined the group. Heidi-Sue was rubbing her hands over Howie's lap, 'massaging his thighs' and saying, 'I never come on to guys, guys always come on to me, I never come on to guys'. Right. Brenna and I had to run off to the kitchen so she didn't catch us choking on laughter.

The crowd was dwindling and the effects of the alcohol and spliffs were taking hold. Beth and Dougie were on the balcony smoking. I perched myself on Norman's knee. Kayla slipped off with the French deejay to another party. Heidi-Sue and Howie disappeared into the guestroom. Josephine had Nez locked into a conversation about zodiac signs. There was a tense moment when the music stopped and Nez knocked on the guestroom door. Heidi-Sue shouted out that he could leave without her, so Josephine took over as Nez' date for the evening and they set off into the night. Rupert snuck off too at some point. Brenna, having been formally introduced to Norman, excused herself soberly to go home to bed. I liked her more all the time. This left Dougie, Beth, Norman, and me sitting around the kitchen table in the aftermath of a terrific party. Dougie persuaded me to join them on the vodka. I sipped mine, hoping it would endear me to Beth somehow.

Looking forward to smoking a pipe of hashish someone had brought him as a present, Norman gave Dougie and Beth his best regards and pardoned himself to bed, telling Dougie he'd lay out bedding if he wanted to crash on the couch. I wished I hadn't agreed to another drink. I was already feeling quite drunk and tired, and really just wanted to curl up in bed. It was odd seeing Dougie with Beth. He was charming and suave, and kind of sexy in a way I'd never really noticed before. Beth was playfully giving him a hard time. I could see that she knew what she was doing so I decided to slip out and leave them alone.

Norman was running a bath as I fell onto our bed. I heard the door to the guestroom open and Heidi-Sue's voice asking, 'Where is everybody?' Then silence. A few minutes later the front door opened and shut carefully. I almost drifted off to sleep when I heard another muffling of voices, drawn out longer than the other pair, and finally the door shutting.

Then a knock at the bedroom door.

"Come in," I said sitting up woozily.

Dougie walked straight over to me. He handed me a crumpled, stained paper napkin, nodding towards it for me to have a look. Holding it close to my eyes in the dim light, I realized what it was: Beth's pledge to invest enough money to at least get Chinatown open.

"This is it? This is it!"

I sprung off the bed leaping into Dougie's arms. He spun me around in circles. This had been the moment we'd been waiting for. Chinatown was going to happen! We both stopped and looked at the napkin again, double-checking that it wasn't a dream. Words can't describe the wave of relief that broke over us.

Throwing open the bathroom door, I entered, Dougie hanging in the doorway behind me. Norman looked up at us from the bathtub where he was wearing his glasses and doing a crossword puzzle.

"What's going on?" he asked.

I held the napkin in front of his face, bouncing up and down. As it sunk in, I could literally see weight lift off his shoulders.

"Ex-cell-ent! This is great news! Congratulations brother!" he said to Dougie. "This is serious you think?"

Dougie nodded with tears in his eyes as he shook Norman's hand.

"Looks like we've got ourselves a nightclub then kids!"

CHAPTER 18 – Showgirl's Guide to the Galaxy

- **Body** – Fake-n-bake. A little bit of a tan goes a long ways in accentuating a fit figure. It makes toned muscles more apparent and conceals signs of cellulite. I recommend a gradual tinting moisturizer, as caution should be taken to avoid the 'Umpa Lumpa' effect from over-application. Doing sit-ups and push-ups right before going on stage swells muscles, making them look instantly more toned. Brown eye-shadow or bronzer can be used to fake muscle definition. I like to rub baby oil on my stomach because it flatters under the lights, but am careful not to get it on costumes, as it ruins elastic. And I can't recommend nude fishnets highly enough. Professional dance fishnets are very robust and worth the investment. And no wedding or engagement rings on stage. Disrupts the fantasy.

- **Hair** – Wigs are a showgirl's best friend, in my opinion. At the beginning of the night, I pin my hair, clean or dirty, under a wig cap. Then I wear half a dozen wigs over the course of an evening, changing characters and personalities with each one. For the right act I'll expose my natural hair as part of the reveal. It makes the audience feel like they've had a glimpse at the real you, and that is very sexy.

• **Hair Removal** – To wax or not to wax? That is the question. One of the most controversial and common dressing room topics. Waxing is probably the best course of action if you can afford it, but shaving is the best way to stay on top of it. Some might argue hair removal lotions are the way to go, but I've also witnessed this technique go disastrously wrong, causing chemical burns that have put girls out of commission for days.

• **Make-up** – Always color in eyebrows and lips a shade darker than natural for the stage. Use brown shadow to define cheekbones, eye-arches and jawline. Eyes should be the main feature. If eyes look tired, a great trick is to apply white shine on the inside corner of the bottom lash line, and under the brow arch. Lots of showgirls love sparkles, but I would advise using sparingly and touching up often. Never use craft sparkles. And be prepared that everyone who you come in contact with for days after will magically acquire your fairy dust. When I lived with Miss Melody Sweets in the East Village, there was so much glitter in our apartment that her cat used to shit glittery poop!

• **Lashes** – Long fake eyelashes are essential. Sometimes I wear two pairs. In photographs you really see the difference they make. It's huge. I recommend lining the eye with pencil or liquid eyeliner first. Then cut lashes to fit your eye. Put a thin line of black Duo eyelash glue on the side of a finger, dip the lashes lightly, count to ten, and then apply to the lid. Hold for several seconds, blink, look, and adjust before they dry. Then you may want to line over the lashes with shadow or a pencil.

• **Shoes** – With an ankle strap. Otherwise you might literally 'break-a-leg'. Nude and gold toned shoes make legs look longer, black shoes make legs look shorter.

• **G-Strings** – Nude. Tiny. Worn under everything. Own several. Cut tags out of everything.

• **Bras** – The smaller the center of a bra is where the two cups connect, the bigger and more accentuated the boobs look. If padding a bra, be sure to secure the padding with double-sided tape, pins or glue.

• **Pasties & Nipple Tassels** – They're the same thing, except Brits think 'pasties' are something you eat. Showgirl's have different preferences in this area, from using double-sided, toupee, or even carpet tape, to eyelash glue and spirit gum. If using glue, apply it to the shape of the pastie and allow it to slightly dry for ten to fifteen seconds before placing on the body. Hold for twenty seconds. After use, peel gently off the breast. Baby oil can help ease this process, as well as applying heat from a hairdryer to gently loosen the adhesive. Clean nipple thoroughly to remove stickiness and residue.

Some people might find it hard to believe, but I've never even tried a pair of pasties on. It's true! When I met Norman he was so saturated in tasseled women that he was completely uninterested in seeing me in a pair. So I've just never tried them. And at this point, it's become sort of a thing, my gimmick. Gypsy Rose Lee never went down to pasties either, and she's regarded as the greatest burlesque artist of all time.

Another reason it's sort of ironic is because I'm the creator of 'Tassology: The World's Largest Pastie Collection, Part IV'. What began as a publicity stunt to spread the word about Chinatown, turned into a wildly popular exhibition at Shanghai's première gallery, Art Labor, and then a permanent display at the club in the second floor hallway. I asked burlesque artists from around the world to donate a pair of worn pasties to be framed and mounted on the wall at China's first burlesque nightclub. Adding them to my own hand-made collection, I had well over a hundred pairs. Antiqued labels had real or invented stage names, followed by the title of the real or invented act the pasties had featured in, with a location and year.

'Bogus archivery', I called it. People didn't question the authenticity of the items, assuming that if it was presented as such, than it must be real. In effect, it made a bigger statement, one that could be applied to China and its vast fake market. In Communist China, my collection was considered risqué, provocative and refreshingly kinky. Just the exhibition on the subject matter alone made more of a statement than it could in many places in the world. I loved that about Shanghai. The art scene in New York never would have given me an opportunity like that.

Chinese art was in the midst of a major boom. For the past decade, the government had been desperate to bolster their self-view as a cultural force, not just the planet's sweatshop. This allowed funding to flow towards their art scene, and artists were taking greater chances, using their brushes as a voice. That is dangerous though because in China there can only be one voice. I think that's why this boom was so exhilarating. It was like everyone was waiting to see how far the bubble could expand, knowing that at some point it had to burst. And everyone I talked to believed that the Chinese would burst its own bubble before anything else did. Art is subjective, seemingly making it defendable, or at least that's the idea. Before any show opens, military censors must approve every piece of the displayed work. Anything deemed questionable must be removed, or else they'll shut the whole exhibition down.

As a fellow artist, I rooted for this freedom, this voice. Yet I was burdened with suspicion that it was just a matter of time before an artist became too famous, or went too far, or said something through art that the-powers-that-be didn't want to hear.

By opening a place like Chinatown and being the one responsible for the show, I was essentially putting myself on the front lines of this precarious artistic movement that was happening- or trying to happen, at least. When I set out on this adventure, it was just that: An adventure. I didn't understand the enormity of the task at hand or what it actually represented politically. I never considered our shows to be political theatre, but the fact that we produced the kind of shows we did in this particular country, at this particular time, definitely tipped it into political territory. In a way, I think we got away with it because we were foreigners. But on the other hand, it worried me, because if a government breakdown or a backlash was to happen, being lǎowài would make us targets.

CHAPTER 19 – Teasing Piers Morgan

The day of our opening, I stood backstage in one of the '6 Terrific Girls' costumes as a sound technician poked a wireless microphone box into the back of my knickers. I could see him contemplating how he was going to secure the tiny microphone between my tits while maintaining a professional distance.

"Having fun there buddy?" I teased. His face turned as pink as my costume.

I was about to be interviewed by a famous television personality from the UK by the name of Piers Morgan. He heard about our club and wanted to feature us as his nightspot destination of choice in a one-hour documentary on Shanghai for British TV. The program would be seen by an estimated hundred million viewers. That's a heck of a lot of people. To be completely honest, I'd never heard of him.

"He's an arrogant fucktard," Rupert told me in his punctuated, sharpened English tongue. "He's famous for being a prick. Don't be fooled. He'll probably start out all suave and charming, but watch out. He'll try to provoke you, asking intrusive questions, and before you know it, he'll have you in tears. Blubbing for the whole world to see."

Good to know. I doubted he was as bad as all that. Rupert has a flare for the dramatic. But I was definitely feeling more nervous now than I was before. I worried that I'd start rattling on. Or worse, freeze up and have nothing to say.

"So what should I do? Do you have any advice for me?" I asked with a fretted brow.

Like a coach, he leaned in, his thin face close to mine. "Be on your guard. Don't let him get the upper hand. Show him whose boss. Who are you?" he barked at me like a drill sergeant.

"I don't know, who am I?"

"You're Miss Amelia!"

"I'm Miss Amelia."

"That's right. He's in your house, you're the boss."

It took me a second, but then it hit me what he was trying to say. I'm Miss Amelia! I could do the interview in character. She's my secret weapon. She's not scared of anything.

The crew scrambled to set up the shot for the interview at the 1st floor bar. Through the velvet curtains, I sauntered on stage. Heads turned like dominos. I'd underestimated the impact of my body in this costume on a bunch of jetlagged Brits. I had definitely made an entrance. I cocked my legs coquettishly as my eyes adjusted to the light. Then I walked into the place like I owned the joint, exuding confidence, glamour, and pizzazz. *I do own this joint.* Oh, yeah. Miss Amelia could bring grown men to their knees. This was going to be fun, I thought as I sashayed to the bar.

A tall, unnaturally tanned and shiny man walked up and stood next to me. He must be the guy. He caught the head bartender's attention.

"I'd like a glass of Dom Perignon."

"Make that two darling." Turning to Piers, I said straightly, "It's on me." He squinted in my direction, resisting his instinct to smile.

"That's not necessary," he said, in a posh Brit accent, a smooth operator indeed.

"Well, if you insist," I conceded. "You must be Mister Morgan."

I offered him my hand to shake. He brought it to his lips and kissed it. I was determined not to let him throw me off my game.

"Please, call me Piers. And you are?"

"Miss Amelia."

"Miss Amelia. That's a lovely name. And what's your real name Miss Amelia?"

"Amelia is my real name. But please, call me Miss Amelia."

My southern belle accent was starting to creep out. Was I taking this sassy attitude thing too far? I'd said it with a twinkling smile and he didn't appear to be offended. Far from it actually. I had his attention now, so I kept talking.

"You're quite the celebrity I hear?" He scoped me out to see if I was joking. My eyebrows assured him I wasn't.

"Yes, you could say that." I think he was perplexed that I didn't recognize him. "Have you ever seen Britain's Got Talent?"

"No, sorry... Censorship," I shrugged. "Why? Are you the host?"

"No, I'm a panelist. One of the judges. It's a talent competition. We had a burlesque act on last season."

"Ha! I bet," I rolled my eyes at how mainstream burlesque must be now in the West to be on a TV talent competition. His eyes looked me up and down.

"So, you're a showgirl?"

"What was your first hint?" I sassed. "I can see you're really good at this whole interviewing thing." He chuckled, slipping a hand down his pocket. I'd made him uncomfortable. This guy wasn't so bad, I thought, I could handle him.

"Well, Miss Amelia, I'm about to interview the owners here in fact…"

What? I almost came back with my first 'Don't you know who I am?' but I thought twice. I wanted to see where he was going with that.

"When I'm finished you should join me in my private booth. We'll have some more champagne." I clinked my glass to his, attaching eyes. I couldn't tell if he was slimy or sweet. Or both. He wasn't un-likable.

"Sure, I'd love for you to buy me a bottle of champagne." The more fresh I was to him, the more interested he was in me.

"It would be my pleasure." He didn't even flinch.

He was whisked away by his handlers and the make-up artist, setting him under the lights for the shoot. Norman came out the stage door and presented himself to the crew, tipping his bowler hat, winking at the ladies. He was dressed in his signature cheeky-chappie style: Spats, vest, pocket-watch, the works. He knew who Piers Morgan was, but wasn't intimidated in the least. Norm took his place in the shot next to Piers, introduced himself and started to interview him. I waited until the last minute to sit down in the shot myself. When I did, Piers did a double-take. I flashed him a saucy smirk. My plan was working.

"Where you from mate?" Norman asked.

"Lewes originally," he obliged, rather uninterested.

"Ah, yes, I know it well. I'm a Bristol boy me-self mate, down dere in the luvverly ole West Country now, 'init I, me babs?"

Norman reserves his regional accent strictly for comedic effect, in contrast to his acquired Queen's English. Born a commoner, the son of a publican, Norman received a scholarship to study at Clifton College where they tried to teach him to behave like the upper classes, before he got kicked out for starting a faction of The Young Anarchist League.

"Where are you from Miss Amelia?"

"Originally Virginia, right outside D.C. Then I moved to New York when I was eighteen, and I've been here in Shanghai for about two years now."

"So that makes you....?" He was after my age.

"Old enough!" I flirted, flipping my hair.

"You've accomplished a lot for being so young. Most people probably assume you just get by on your looks."

"Is that what they say about you?" I retorted. Norman winced, Piers laughed, then held his glass up to me.

"Brains and beauty... my favorite combination." He took a sip of bubbly.

"Watch it Morgan, that's my wife you're talking to," Norman cautioned.

Champagne sprayed out of Piers' mouth across the floor. The make-up artist came over to re-powder his chin. He smiled like the story had just gotten interesting. With the mood set, it was time to begin.

Most of his questions were directed towards Norman who had a witty response to everything.

"Do you plan to single-handedly bring back the glamour to Shanghai?"

"No mate, I plan on using both my hands. Going to wash them first though."

"So you consider yourself to be the high-end of the racy market?"

"Thank you very much."

"Are you aware of Shanghai's historic reputation as 'The Paris of the East', a virtual fleshpot?"

"Back in the day there was a notorious nightclub called The Great World. It was constructed on six floors, and as you ascended, each floor got saucier and naughtier."

"What happened at the top?"

"We plan to open the seventh floor."

After awhile of patiently sitting there, looking back and forth between the two men, it was finally my turn.

"That brings me around to you Miss Amelia... May I first say, you look ravishing this evening."

I thanked him passively. Come on, get on with it.

"So would you say that you're probably the naughtiest girl in Shanghai?"

Really? That's what you got? If he was going to throw me questions like that, he was begging to be put in his place. Two can play at this game.

"Sorry to disappoint you Piers, but I'm far from being the naughtiest girl in Shanghai, as you put it. I'm the director of the show here, as well as a performer. My background is in theatre, I grew up on stage and studied Shakespeare at Oxford. So while what I produce here at Chinatown is intended to titillate and exhilarate, I'm more interested in provoking and teasing someone's imagination, which I find, and I believe our audiences would agree, is far sexier, and maybe even filthier, than simply the exposure of flesh."

Take that.

We continued on in this fashion. He'd deliver questions that were meant to make me look like a bimbo, and I'd turn them around, giving eloquent and sophisticated answers, being sure to point out areas in which he'd been misinformed. He seemed to be getting a kick out of my feisty replies.

"And what do you two say to people who don't think a burlesque nightclub in The People's Republic of China is possible?"

"It's not!" Norman and I said, answering and laughing in unison.

Needless to say, most of my finest replies got cut from the show, and many of Norman's best lines were repeated by Piers and edited to come out of his mouth instead. Afterwards, Piers told us that he couldn't remember the last time he enjoyed doing an interview that much. We'd given him a run for his money, something he clearly wasn't used to.

A little while later as I prepared for the evening in the dressing room, I received a present from a secret admirer: A bottle of Dom Perignon. Someone's imagination had certainly been teased.

CHAPTER 20 – Raising the Red Curtain

It had arrived: Gosney & Kallman's Chinatown was finally opening. My hands shook in my white, silk opera gloves as I peeked through the curtain. The place was packed. People had flown in from all over the world and were dressed to the nines in tuxedos, evening gowns and couture fabric-market designs created especially for the occasion. I still couldn't get my head around the fact that I – a young, middle-class, white girl from Virginia - owned a nightclub. And not just any old nightclub, but a burlesque club - in China! It was too good to be true.

The night before the opening I couldn't sleep, and that day I couldn't eat, feeling sick with nerves. Everyone had been coming up to me all day asking questions I pretended to know the answers to, but half the time I was just making them up. I didn't have all the answers. I'd been holding these feelings down, hiding them under a plastered smile, hoping that no one would see the terror in my eyes. I didn't even know what I was so afraid of. The show was in great shape, I was really proud of it, and the club...

Norman had really outdone himself. Chinatown was the quintessential picture of a dream-come-true nightclub, like the ones that only truly existed in old black and white movies, but this was the real thing. The stunning Deco meets temple structure of the main room, now predominantly a deep, sensual scarlet, had been adorned and accentuated with all the tones and textures of Music Hall at its peak. Overlooked by nine individually styled private boxes, tricked out in Victorian splendor with flocked wallpapers and dazzling brocades, the main floor tables were packed with an anxious crowd. The tables and banquets faced an imposing proscenium stage, with lavish curtains and decorative plasterwork, flanked to the left by the emcee's pulpit, and to the right by a separate, thrust stage for the jazz band. Aspidistras and frond palms added a period lushness; rich drapes dropped the full fifteen meters from the barreled ceiling.

On the mezzanine behind the boxes, a separate level with its own bar, gallery and bathrooms, led to a third floor VIP bar, set high in the heavens of the arched structure. Norman kept the arched, triangular flying buttresses exposed, accentuating the building's unique, raw structural beauty in rustic gold. The arch theme echoing the building's façade was used throughout, from the outer frame of the private boxes to the proscenium itself. Mirrors, eclectic treasures, and selections of rare, scavenged, vintage photographs and posters adorned the walls. Opulent and elegant, Chinatown truly was Norman's crowning masterpiece.

As I made my way upstairs towards the tech booth to go over some last minute changes with Claude, I squeezed through the rowdy crowd. The club was in full swing with the jazz quartet playing on the band platform under the romantic yellow light from a built-in streetlamp on the stage. One showgirl worked the room on stilts, whipping optical lights above heads, while another did tricks hanging from an aerial hoop. Waitresses pushed dessert carts, cigarette girls sold merchandise, and champagne corks popped through the air. A photographer called my name, cameras flashed in my eyes and the people around me shouted their congratulations over the music. Smiling and overwhelmed, I continued to push through to the 2nd floor until I faced the ladder up to the crow's nest tech booth. I took off my stilettos and hiked up my silver sparkling, low-cut evening gown, and precariously climbed up the ladder as a customer below whistled at me.

"Here, let me help you," Claude offered his hand. "Wow," he said as I readjusted myself, "I've never seen you look so…"

"So girlie?"

"Yeah. You… look great."

The words flushed across my face and he looked down too, pushing his glasses back up his nose, and we stood embarrassed for a second like school kids on a playground. He offered me a beer. He had come prepared, bringing his own stash in a cooler. He popped one open and made me sit down. He was remarkably calm considering that everyone else in the club was running around like headless chickens. He was always telling me that I was 'too grown up' and needed to relax more, so when he invited me to come hear him deejay the following week at Logo, I agreed.

We went over the last minute changes and I reminded him again about what to do should the police come. Because Claude didn't have a work visa, and

Benny Sideways didn't have a performance license, they would both have to leave the club immediately if the cops showed up for any reason, or else we would face huge fines and serious consequences. Norman had a secret trapdoor built into the back of the stage leading to a tunnel that let out onto an ally, which they would use to get out of the club unseen if necessary. Claude said it was kind of fun to practice the escape, but the tunnel smelled dank like a sewer.

The Cultural Bureau had given me their word that I could get away with showing some sexy flesh on stage that night. I had a grace period to present what I deemed appropriate as far as stripping and nudity was concerned. If they disagreed with my taste, then I'd be required to make changes. I figured that if I could make it through the initial round of scrutiny, then it would give me freedom to take more chances later on. Anyways, I was saving the dirty, too-hot-for-primetime stuff for our late-night after-parties in the third floor VIP bar. From the tech booth, I could look right across into the lofted lounge. There hadn't been a third floor bar in the original design, but it was Norman's answer to losing that chunk of 2nd floor real estate to the brothel next door.

One number I was real excited to present that evening was 'The Robber Burlesque', a perfect example of new-vaudeville meets burlesque, meets China. It was first imagined because I wanted to see if I could possibly work Chairman Mao into a burlesque routine and get away with it. This got me thinking about an interior of a home as a set, with a window and door on the back wall and a framed picture of Chairman Mao hung between them. In many homes a picture of Mao is a common feature, even to this day. The premise of the act was a robber, played by Benny Sideways, sneaks into a lady's house while she's out. He goes for her diamonds, sniffs her panties, sprays musk, and basks stupidly in the scent. Suddenly, the music signals a change and Josephine can be seen through the window arriving home, looking in her purse for keys. Benny drops his sack panicking, looks around for a place to hide, backs up against the wall, lifting the frame off of the Chairman Mao picture, and takes his place as the portrait behind the picture frame. His clothes closely match the colors of the wall, camouflaging him, like a Looney Tunes cartoon.

The music changes as Josephine comes flouncing in, full of burly-Q glamour. Throwing her leopard print fur coat and her turkey feather hat off, exhausted from a night out on the town. She begins to undress for bed. She strips down to her bra and panties, not noticing that the burglar is watching her every move, hilariously trying his hardest to control his arousal. She unsnaps her bra, takes off both straps, and then notices the sack on the ground. She looks up, then slowly turns around. She spots him! Throwing her hands into the air she drops her bra screaming, revealing her bare breasts to lucky Benny Sideways and only her bare back to the audience, allowing us to just get away with the nudity. She covers herself, gives him a proper ass-kicking and kinky spanking, before the fight moves behind a dressing screen. Arms and clothes fly, and when they come back out, she's wearing his clothes and he's in his underpants, running out the door defeated. The chick always comes out on top in my shows, no exceptions.

Having slugged down my beer, I was definitely feeling slightly more relaxed. Back down on the 2nd floor, Norman stood in a tuxedo at the service bar telling a crowd about the history of the building. When he saw me he excused himself. He reached for my hand and told me he wanted to show me something, leading me over to the private balcony by our small office. It was the best view of the whole club and he wanted me to take it all in.

"We've actually done it," he said, not completely believing it either.

He pointed out our VIP guests situated in our private booths: Gage, our personal favorite VIP, was amongst friends in the Absinthe Room; Andy Lau, a famous Hong Kong movie star in the Champagne Room; Miss China in the Opal Room; Miss Hong Kong in the Lover's Box; and the contractor Harley Zhou with Remco Bredenberg and his wife, our secretary, Goldfish, and the government officials occupied the Red Rum Room. I'd named that one after the red elaborate, flocked, Victorian wallpaper, but every time Norman or I said it we couldn't resist giving it a go in our best *The Shining* voices. Our Chinese wait staff must have thought we were crazy.

Turning to Norman, I thanked him sincerely for making this dream come true.

"Hey, you don't need to thank me. You've worked just as hard for this as I have." He went on to tell me that his shows had never looked so good before and that was down to me. The best compliment I could ask for.

"Well it's like you said," I told him, "We're in this thing together."

His hand slid through the slit of my dress, caressing my thigh. There he discovered that I was wearing stockings and a garter, part the outfit he bought me for my birthday, mail-ordered from Agent

Provocateur. It was the nicest lingerie I owned. I told him I would show him the whole works if he wanted to 'step into my office'.

About ten minutes later, we emerged from the office back into the club straightening our clothes, and declaring it time to start the show. Looking across the balconies one last time, something caught my eye. It was one of the showgirls in the government booth. Heidi-Sue. She was in her showgirl costume drinking champagne and flirting with Remco right in front of Remco's wife and the government officials we were trying so hard to impress. My stomach flopped as I went to retrieve her.

"You know that Remco's wife was right there, right?"

She just laughed and said, "Don't you worry your pretty little head about me girlie. I've been around the block a few times, I know what I'm doing."

No doubt. I bit my lower lip and kept walking.

Backstage, Freddy was doing his vocal warm ups as Rupert glared at him, shining his shoes. The smell of garlic broccoli wafted through the air and I called out to no one in particular, "I thought we agreed no garlic broccoli backstage!"

Kayla tapped me on the shoulder.

"Amelia!" She had a shred of alarm in her voice. She leaned in to whisper in my ear, "Star's locked herself in the bathroom and won't come out. She says she can't go on."

Geez Louise.

"Okay. Okay.... It'll be okay, don't worry," I told her, telling myself at the same time. "I'll talk to her. Go finish getting ready, I want to start in ten."

I shooed her away, so she wasn't breathing down my neck. I needed to think. What tactic should I use, I wondered. Should I be forceful and say 'This is your boss speaking,' or just talk to her as my friend? I took a deep breath. Okay, I was just going to go for it. I tip-toed backwards a few feet, then sprang forward, jogging, pegging the floor in my heels, then banged hard on the door.

"Oh my god, I'm going to be sick! I'm going to throw up! All over the place! Please open the door!"

Maybe it wasn't the classiest tactic, but the door did fling open and Star jumped out of my way. I entered the small bathroom and shut the door behind me. We stood there looking at each other.

"Hey," I eventually said. The tiny bathroom was filled with cigarette smoke. She sat back down on the toilet lid and took out another one. She lit up, inhaled deep, then exhaled.

"Can I have one?" I asked. She looked at me, knowing I'd quit, and I could see her almost turn me down, but then she took the one out of her mouth and handed it to me, lighting another one up for herself.

I took a long drag. Breaking the silence, I finally asked, "Are you mad at me?"

Last night in rehearsal I cut the act she starred in, the most ambitious number in the show, 'Shanghai Lil'. It was a difficult number because it involved precise timing and interacting with film, as well as a live song, dance and stage fight. The cast had rallied though and came in early that morning to work on it. Satisfied that it was audience ready, I'd put it back in the show at the last minute.

"No," she said. "I only feel sick. I don't know why."

"Are you afraid?"

"I never get fear before show, but I have. I have fear." She smacked her forehead into her hands.

"I have fear too."

With a sudden head rush, I looked at the burning cherry, thinking about all the moments in my life that had been punctuated with a cigarette, then stubbed it out. Star looked at me with her violet eyes.

"You are not from here," she said. "I am from here. What if no one likes? I like, but Chinese people, she is very..." she couldn't find her words. "She might not understand. And maybe she look at me and think, oh, she is bad girl. She does bad things with foreigners. She is not good Chinese."

I didn't know what to say. I'd been so caught up in my own world that I never stopped to think about what a big deal this must be for her. What if the Chinese didn't like it? I'd gone out of my way to make a show that I thought would appeal to them, but seeing Star so worried frightened me. But I couldn't let myself go there. It was too late.

"Sweetheart," I said firmly, aware that it was the moment when I was required to give the pep talk of a lifetime, while carefully walking that tightrope between friend and boss. "No one is going to think you are a bad girl. If they think anyone is a bad girl, it'll be me, okay? Or Miss Pinky."

That made her laugh. She'd never gotten along with the other local girl.

"And if they don't like it tonight - which they will - then we'll just have to change it, okay? But please believe me when I say this: What we have here, Chinatown, you, The Dolls - it's really world class. There's no one else on earth doing what we're about to do here tonight. This is bigger than all of us. And if we're going to go down in history, you want to be remembered for shining brightly, don't you?"

I hoped I was saying the right things, these kinds of speeches didn't come naturally to me. I stepped towards her and took her hand. She was coming around, I could tell.

"I need you. The other girls need you too," I mouthed. "We're a team." I pulled her onto her feet. "So let's go out there and kick some ass, okay? Are you with me?"

Star nodded. She was with me. We hugged tightly, until she pulled away and said in perfectly clear English, "I think you are my sister." My heart throbbed, completely touched, knowing that was one of the highest compliments anyone could get from a Chinese girl. In that moment my nerves evaporated and I knew that, whatever happened, everything was going to be okay.

When we started to walk back to the dressing room I asked, "Have you ever heard of an actor, I think his name is Andy Lau?"

"Yes, he is very famous."

"Oh. Well, he's here tonight."

She stopped dead in her tracks and looked at me to see if I was serious. I indicated I was. Then she screamed at the top of her lungs. Scared the living daylights outta me. I thought something was terribly wrong, but no - it was just Andy Lau mania. Apparently, he's like the Brad Pitt of Chinese cinema. I wondered if it was a mistake to have told her, I didn't want her to lock herself in the bathroom again, but after she settled down - a little - she transformed into Dance Captain dictator. Clapping her hands she ordered the showgirls into places. Now Star was determined to shine her brightest out there. She was out to bag herself a movie star.

CHAPTER 21 – Chinese Whispers

Our first show was almost over. By the second part, the show had really hit its groove. The girls were into it and had the confidence I'd been waiting for, and the crowd seemed to be having a ball. I'd been going back and forth from hosting the front of house with Norman, mingling with the customers and schmoozing with officials, to backstage, giving feedback, reminders and encouragement. Freddy was doing his final set before our finale when I ducked backstage to congratulate the girls on a job well done.

As I crept through the wings and past the wall of Freddy's crooning, I could hear violent shrieks and shouts coming from the girl's dressing room. I ran until I pushed through the cast in the doorway to see Star and Pinky in their Can Can costumes pulling each other's hair out. They fell to the floor, wrestling. I shouted at them to stop and grabbed Star by the shoulders to separate the two girls. From several feet away Pinky spit in Star's direction, but she moved and instead of it hitting Star, the spit landed directly in my eye.

Silence.

They waited for my reaction. Kayla handed me a tissue and I sat down on a chair. Freddy's voice could be heard faintly once again. It was his next to last song.

"What happened?" I managed finally.

"He started it," Star said.

"I am a 'she', you stupid dog!" Pinky screeched. "Ni Xi Sun Dian!"

"Pinky! You can't talk to a co-worker like that," I said, defending Star.

"She is a peasant. Look at her skin. Her father works in factory. I should be Dance Captain, not her! I am more better than Star. And her English is so bad. She is so stupid, she cannot understand."

"That's enough." I don't get mad often, so when I do – watch out.

"I don't care. I not want to work with stupid peasant dogs. I will stay but she has to go." The room filled with thick silence as everyone held their breath and Freddy could be heard starting his final song. I counted to ten before I spoke.

"Okay Pinky. You're fired. Pack your things and get out of here."

"What? You may not fire me. I am best dancer here!"

"Not anymore."

I stood up and crossed my arms. Everyone appeared to be in a state of shock. Pinky couldn't believe it either, but when she could, she started throwing a tantrum like a two-year-old: Banging the make-up table, tossing her wigs and costumes on the floor, pretending to bawl fake tears. Everyone just stared. I started to fix my make-up as if I wasn't bothered. Finally, after a dramatic performance, Pinky stormed out. The room exhaled.

I clapped my hands, "The show must go on people. We're almost there."

"But what about The Can Can? Now we're a girl short. What do we do?"

There was only one thing we could do. I picked up Pinky's discarded Can Can costume from the floor and began to put it on.

"What's going on?" Norman said, entering the dressing room. "Why did Pinky just leave in the middle of a show?"

"I fired her," I replied flatly, pulling pink fishnet stockings up my leg.

"You fired her? In the middle of a show?"

That's what I just said, so I didn't bother answering.

"And what are you doing now? You can't go on."

"Watch me," I said, pinning the tiny top hat into my hair. "Let's go girls."

A minute later we rushed the stage, hands on hips, yelling and whooping with feathers and rhinestones flying, like rave meets Victorian harlots. I took Pinky's spot, center stage. All signs of the scene before erased from our faces, replaced with utter dazzling glee. I gave it everything I had, making it look like I'd done it a million times before. My eyes found Norman, who was looking at me like he'd never seen me dance before.

Something caught my eye near the door. A flood of men - men in uniform - crowding into the entrance. The door-girl tried to stop them, but it was no use. I must be imagining things, I thought. There was no way this was happening tonight, at our opening, with all the powerful people we had there. Following my eyes, Norman turned to look, right as the police started to approach the front of the stage. Remco and Goldfish were already on the situation, animatedly conversing with the police, demanding to know what the problem was.

It was the end of the number. The bows. Rupert began to introduce the girls one by one.

"Give it up for Miss Shanghai Lil, Miss Ginger Knight, Miss Reina Sunshine, Miss - "

I wasn't there.

"Miss Lavender Chase, and Miss Sassafras! Ladies and Gentleman, The Chinatown Dolls!"

Despite the police presence, the crowd stood up and clapped hard. The girls kicked their final kick line as I walkie-talkie'd Claude in the tech booth to get his butt down here. The cast piled off stage when the curtain closed, and we huddled over the trapdoor in the floor as Benny opened it, just like we practiced.

"What's going on?" Freddy asked me.

"I don't know, but the police are here. Benny doesn't have a performance license and Claude doesn't have a work permit so they need to get out of here before we all get in trouble. Where is he? Do you have the flashlights?" Brenna handed them to Benny. Norman came rushing backstage.

"Good," he said looking at Benny, who was waist deep in the hole. "Where's Claude?"

Claude came tearing around the bend.

"They're right behind me," he said as he jumped down the trapdoor. We shut the lid just as the police came through the curtains.

Sound violations. They got us on sound violations, Remco reported, before he took the Chief of Police out to a KTV to try and save face and smooth things over. Norman had gone outside with the cops to see their decibel meter for himself and it was true. We were way over the noise limit. They made us shut the music off. They didn't make us kick people out, but after that night we wouldn't be allowed to open again until further notice. Shutdown on our opening night. It was unbelievable.

The audience, drunk and oblivious to the seriousness of the situation, ate it up like it was part of the entertainment. Norman, Beth and I huddled in a corner backstage, hiding out and trying to think our way around the mess. How was this even possible? This can't be true. Then Dougie burst around the corner. His shirt was untucked and he had lipstick on his cheeks. It was the first time any of us had seen him since the beginning of the night.

"Guys, what happened? Is everything okay?"

We were speechless for a moment, unsure of how to even begin to answer that question. He looked around for a chair, moving on an uncoordinated diagonal, rather intoxicated. Norman filled him in about what went down, but Dougie got agitated and wanted to know why no one came to get him from the VIP bar. Norman told him that it was a good thing he hadn't gotten him because he was obviously drunk. Dougie denied it. Then Norman said something to the effect of, 'When people drink, they get stupid,' and Dougie thought he was calling him stupid. That's when Dougie kicked the chair out from under himself and aggressively stood over Norman. It was intended as a threat. Norman sprang to his feet. Beth begged them to stop. Norman told her to stay out of it. That infuriated Dougie and the next thing we knew, Dougie's knuckles were coming straight for Norman's head. He ducked and Dougie's fist went straight through the wall.

Slowly, he took his hand back out, cradled it in pain. He headed towards the bar to get some ice. Norman inspected the hole he left in the wall. And then a light bulb went off over his head:

No insulation.

There was no sound insulation in the wall. Used to dealing with New York's draconian sound level restrictions, Norman had designed a very specific, multi-layered configuration of acoustic foam and baffleboard. It needed to be installed just so, in order to fulfill its objective. But instead, there was nothing. He was furious. No wonder we had sound violations. Harley's construction team had explicit instructions. So this wouldn't happen. Harley had given Norman his word. Now what were we going to do?

CHAPTER 22 – Up Against the Great Wall

In Dougie's office, I sat making phone calls. Dougie wasn't there, he'd gone to Sydney. Norman received a phone call from him the day after they nearly came to blows, offering an indirect apology and telling him that his kid sister tried to commit suicide over the weekend. She was alive, but Dougie was getting on a plane to go be with his family. He wasn't sure when he would be coming back. We sent our best wishes. Consequently though, I got stuck with the job of organizing our company's Golden Week party.

Golden Week is an October holiday that gives people seven continuous days off work. The holiday was made-up in 1999 to encourage domestic tourism. It's estimated that over 120 million people travel during that time and the city virtually shuts down. It was expected of us to host a banquet for our Chinese employees in honor of this bogus occasion. We were keeping our fingers crossed that not too many of them would quit during the delay because we were finding out that good employees were hard to come by in Shanghai.

Getting foreigners to participate in a ritualistic night of Chinese-style partying wasn't easy either. People suddenly got very busy, were out of town or came down with vague, mysterious, and likely imaginary, illnesses.

"Come on, it'll be fun!" I tried my best to convince them. "Free food, karaoke… free drinks. It's Golden Week!"

I'd taken it upon myself to keep everyone's spirits up during the enforced hiatus, trying to project consistent positivity. Funny, but I too had adopted the concept of *face*.

The truth was, there had been nothing even remotely golden about my week. By the day following the opening, after further walls were opened and Harley the contractor summoned, we had a full picture of the situation. Harley grudgingly admitted to not installing the insulation, blaming his workers to save face. It was calculated it would take two weeks to get the work done, and at least another two to get the requisite paper trail in order before we could reopen.

That meant there would be a minimum of a month of no business, yet full bills. Our initial debut was now on ice, our carefully calculated PR campaign losing impetus. Opening a nightclub, especially one with a show, is like bringing a kettle to boil, and you really want to keep it hot. This closing meant we lost our head of steam, our forward motion delayed. And as Norman was beginning to go through the details to turn the situation around, we now had standing staff of over sixty with contracts already operative. You expect to haul in big money in your first month open, even if the place is rubbish, everyone will want to check it out. We weren't rubbish, and everyone really did want to check us out, but now we would all have to wait. And with the delay came a whole new wave of bribes to pay, and I don't have to remind anyone that *bribes cost money*. It sounds bad, right? But wait, there's more.

Earlier that week, Beth got a phone call from the Mayor's wife who had attended our opening. She told Beth that she and her husband loved the club and couldn't wait to come back, but 'there's something you should know'. At the end of the night, the waitress presented them with a bill on a piece of cardboard, requesting a twenty percent service charge of two hundred kwai. Their drinks and fruit platters were complimentary, so she thought that was bizarre. It was. We knew nothing about this Beth assured her, apologizing profusely and offering her full compensation.

When we confronted the waitress, she giggled and covered her mouth with her hand. We had learned by then that this was a sure tell that a local person was lying. She was fired on the spot and Beth notified the police. Within twenty-four hours we were informed that the fired, thieving employee was suing us for the full payment of her mandated six-month contract. Apparently this is possible, common even. Our lawyer advised us to settle out of court, explaining that she would win the lawsuit simply because she's a local Chinese and we are not. That really pissed me off. It made me feel like they're all in some kind of Chinese conspiracy against foreigners. It just wasn't right.

On top of everything else, I needed to find a new stage manager. I had hired Heidi-Sue and Josephine's friend, the Cameroonian guy, Nez, to be our stage manager, but now he was out, and under really disturbing circumstances too. I thought there was something weird about him when we were rehearsing 'I'm Tired,' from Mel Brook's *Blazing Saddles* and I had brought Nez in to learn the boy's song and dance routine as a sort of audition. While he looked great in the male chorus line, adding to our United Nations appeal, I discovered that, despite claims, he couldn't carry a tune. I encouraged him to work on it, chalking it up to nerves, but at the next rehearsal he'd forgotten the choreography, hadn't worked on the song, and then he even tried to hit on me. We used our limited number of performance licenses as an excuse not to include him in the show, but he was so upset we offered him stage manager as a consolation, since he really wanted to be involved and we needed one at that point anyways, and he already had a work visa.

He was supposed to come into the club to help us hang two, forty-foot drops of red, velvet curtains to cover the speakers on either side of the stage, but he didn't show. It wasn't until the next day when Norman and I were both up ladders, laying the gold-plated trim on the top edge of the stage proscenium when he turned up. He asked to have a private word with Norman.

About ten minutes later, Norman said, "Amelia, come here please."

I didn't like the tone of his voice. He hardly ever calls me Amelia. I racked my brain, wondering if I was in trouble for something, but nothing came to mind. I joined them in a banquet and took a seat. Nez looked like crap. He was usually well put together, but today he had red bags under his eyes like he hadn't slept, and his black, African skin looked splotchy and stressed. A hesitation sat in the air. The suspense was making me anxious. I figured he must be quitting, but surely that didn't warrant the weight of this heavy, somber mood.

"What's up?" I asked, breaking the silence.

"Tell her," Norman prodded gently.

It took him awhile to start. It looked like it hurt him to speak. Something must really be wrong. Had someone died?

"The night before last, I go to Logo, then I go to Dada," he began in his Cameroonian accent. "There I met a Mexican girl. She was... visiting. I had too much to drink and she did too." He exhaled audibly. I sat forward in my chair so I could hear him better. "We started kissing, then went back to my place. She say she got a boyfriend in Mexico and this, what we do, is wrong. But she keep kissing me."

I had no idea where he was going with this or why he was confessing these intimate details.

"So we get to my place and start to... to have sex," he lowered his voice. "I flipped her over and... She take the iron from beside the bed and she hit me in the head with it." He took off his baseball cap, showing us a white bandage plastered to his forehead.

"So you were having sex and then all of a sudden she hit you? With an iron?"

I was struggling to understand how it went from Point A to Point B. He just nodded, put his cap back on and continued.

"Blood, it go everywhere. I go to the toilet, outside my room and she slammed the door, locks me out. Then I heard glass break..."

His words were getting harder to regurgitate and his phrases became chopped.

"The only glass in the room is the door to outside, and I try to make her let me in. But then I hear nothing. I kick the door.... and... and..." he began to cry, trying hard not to. "She was gone. I look over the balcony, and down there, there she was."

"Oh my god!" One hand covered my mouth, the other to my head, feeling the virtual impact for myself.

"She jumped?" I whispered. He half nodded, half shrugged.

"What floor do you live on?"

"Eight."

Fucking hell. He said there were people down there who called an ambulance. He panicked and went to McDonald's, and then to the police station about an hour later. She wasn't dead. At least not yet. If she did survive there was the possibility she would be brain damaged. Her parents were flying over from Mexico and, at the moment, no one was pressing any charges. He said that because he's African and the girl's Mexican, the police were acting like they didn't care. He says the Chinese don't like black people, and it seemed like they don't care much for Mexicans either. Had either of them been Chinese, this story would've been much different. It would've been headline news. I was stunned, speechless.

Nez was too afraid to tell the cops that he worked as an English teacher as he had lied about his qualifications to get the job, so he told them he worked for us. Great. Not what we needed, especially right then. The incident had happened in Hongkou too, the same district as Chinatown, meaning more unwanted attention from the local police on our club. I glanced at Norman. His eyes confirmed that our thoughts were aligned. We had to let Nez go. I'd never trust him again after hearing all that. Even if his recollection of the incident was the truth, something didn't add up. We advised him to leave the country as soon as possible in case the girl died and someone changed their mind about pressing charges.

Norman told him firmly, "You do not want to be facing rape and murder charges in China. You'll never get out alive."

Sinking into the leather couch at the KTV, I squeezed between Kayla and Brenna, still stuffed from the twenty-course Golden Week meal. We ate at a restaurant on Zhapu Lu where I watched two of our local staff fight over who got to eat the last fish eye. Yum. The eyes are considered the best part of the fish apparently. One of the waitresses told me, 'They go pop in your mouth.' I took her word for it.

The guys tried to eat the dish 'Drunken Crayfish'. They triple-dog-double-dared me to try a drunken crayfish too, and I hate to turn down a dare, but after Benny Sideways said he could feel it trying to crawl back up his throat, and almost gagged right there at the table, I decided it wasn't worth the glory.

At the KTV, Kayla and I declared ourselves drunk enough to participate in karaoke and we busted out some hardcore Linkin Park. Who knew? And the Acid Pony boys took turns singing Michael Jackson songs while I beat-boxed on the mic. Again... Who knew? But our stage had been high-jacked by the local girls, eager to reclaim the true spirit of karaoke, which we were clearly making a disgrace of. The local girls sing the same sickeningly saccharine sweet, Party approved, sappy love songs, over and over again. They each take a crack at the same tune too, trying to out-emote each other. One girl even burst into tears and couldn't finish, which won her massive approval ratings amongst her peers. They take this stuff pretty seriously. There aren't many outlets for people to express themselves or their individuality, so KTV is where it all comes out.

I watched Freddy waltzing with Star as I took a drag off Kayla's cigarette and said, "Hey, I have to go to the fabric market tomorrow, want to come? I have to pick out the fabric for The Frug costumes for the HK gig."

The only bright side of this enforced interim period was it meant that we were freed up to do a profitable gig for a vodka company in Hong Kong.

"I thought Heidi-Sue was doing them?" Kayla said. Brenna leaned in to hear what we were saying.

"No. She gave Norman and me a budget proposal, but she was way too expensive. Her prices were Western prices, about triple what I know I can get them done for at my local tailor's or the fabric market. And she wanted us to pay her four hundred kwai an hour. That's like over sixty USD. We can't afford to do a show like ours here if we're paying inflated US prices. That's part of the reason we're doing it here, we can afford the lavish costumes and sets... I'm sorry, it's just ridiculous."

"Yeah it is," Brenna rolled her eyes. She didn't like Heidi-Sue. Never did. Says she has 'negative energy'.

"Don't tell anyone I told you that," I added. "Her designs were good, they were. And I know she's having a rough time right now with the divorce and home schooling her kid. Did she tell you why she finally took him out of the Chinese elementary school?"

They both shook their heads. "In his textbook it says that the Chinese were the first people on the moon. Seriously – in a school textbook. Can you believe it?"

"But wait," Kayla turned to me and sat up straight. "Heidi-Sue told me yesterday that she had just met with Beth, and Beth approved her to do The Frug costumes."

"What? That's crazy," I said dismissively. "We turned her down last week."

"That's what she told me."

My eyes narrowed. If she had gone to meet with Beth after Norman and I had given her a definite 'No', then that was pretty messed up.

"I don't think she would do that," I said, sipping my drink. Or would she?

CHAPTER 23 – Chasing the Dragon

Coming home from the gym, I walked into the entryway of our apartment tower and the rank smell of cat piss made me gag. What the hell does that woman have in those bags outside her door that stinks this whole building up something horrible? We'd complained to our landlord about it before. He said nothing could be done because the crazy cat lady comes from a 'noble family'. Not today she don't. I'd had enough. I crammed my bicycle between the others, setting off a droning motorbike alarm. Slamming my backpack down on the stairs, I decided that all this noble woman's stinking cat shit was going in the trash, and I didn't care if The Party spy saw me or not.

I picked up the orange plastic bag on top of a pile that had been sat there for over a week. Without thinking, I looked inside. It took a second to make out the half eaten face of a dead cat swarming in maggots, swimming through eye sockets. Dropping the bag, I tackled my stomach, dry heaving, closing my eyes trying to erase what I'd seen, elbow over my nose. I picked it back up at arms length and ran with it out to the garbage, throwing it in the bin, puke rising up the back of my throat. Seriously… What the fuck? Was she saving it for later? The spy came out of her cave to see what I was doing. She shouted something in Chinese, which I didn't understand and ignored anyways. As I went back into the building, I was welcomed by the immediate nasal relief of just cat piss, rather than dead cat *and* cat piss. Having battled enough for one day, I picked up my bag and trudged up the stairwell in what felt like the longest part of the journey home.

I went straight into the bedroom to change clothes. I could hear Howie and Norman talking in the kitchen. Yes, Howie was still here.

"So I was talking with T.J., you know, that sax player in the quartet?" Howie said to Norman, in his cigarette toasted, Angelino voice.

"Yeah, I know T.J., I introduced you."

"So he says that when Harry Connick Jr. was in town the government was so afraid because of Björk's 'Free Tibet' shit that when he got here they handed him a list of ten songs that he was 'allowed' to play. He didn't have the sheet music for half of them, and none of them were off the album he was trying to promote. Since when did Harry Connick Jr. become a threat to society? Has he gone hardcore or something and I don't know about it?"

"Yeah, Björk really screwed things up here."

This issue of Tibet has been a global controversy for years. In my opinion, China will never give it up. When Björk came to Shanghai and did a concert she sang the song 'Declare Independence', and afterwards yelled, 'Tibet! Tibet!' It is safe to say that China will never invite Björk back again after that.

"We've been directly affected by it," Norman told him. "Because of that, they've tightened up on performance licenses for foreigners. We have to take full legal responsibility for anything said or done on our stage. So basically, if someone did that at our club, I'd be the one to go to jail."

"So tell me about Heidi-Sue." I could almost hear Norman roll his eyes through the wall. Here we go, I thought.

"Not much to tell, mate."

Good answer. He knew better than to get involved in Howie's bizarre sex life, and Heidi-Sue was not our favorite person at the moment. Upon further inspection it had turned out that it was true, she had gone behind our backs to get the money from Beth to do the costumes, after we had blatantly turned her down. Beth told us that Heidi-Sue threatened to quit if she didn't get to do the costumes. We were still trying to measure our response.

"I fucked her again last night," Howie proudly declared. I grimaced at the unwanted visual in my head. There was always one showgirl...

"Howie, please, can we not go there," Norman begged.

"Like fucking a mayonnaise jar."

He was going there.

In my right breast I had been experiencing a sharp, concerning pain. So bad that I couldn't sleep on that side of my body. In the past, for things like a swollen eye, I had just gone to the Chinese doctor's office, as China has national healthcare, and to be seen at a Western hospital where they speak English was six-hundred kwai. For this particular problem, I decided to look into Traditional Chinese Medicine as a more affordable alternative. Dr. Kao, a recommended TCM doctor, came to my house for a three-hour examination, diagnoses and treatment. For an hour and a half I laid nude on my bed in a peaceful trance, first on my front, then on my back. She laid her hands all over my body, doing something between reiki and massage. Then she asked me to come-to so she could explain what she found before continuing.

Skeptically, I hadn't told her why I asked her to come. When the first words out of her mouth were, 'Your pain in your right breast is related to menstruation, which will come in three days', I was impressed. My girlfriends who had been seen by the doctor warned me that she was going to say that I have to get more sleep, drink more water and shouldn't be drinking so much alcohol. That's what I was prepared for. I was absolutely not prepared for what she said next.

"You have a very large tumor deep inside your left breast that is not good. Cancer maybe. I can't tell for sure. Too big for me to fix. You must go to Western doctor and they take out, but you must go to them."

My heart stopped. My mind, a blank, white noise. For the next hour and a half she used something like a thick stick of burning sage held close to my skin. I'd signal when it got too hot, and then she rubbed the area hard with the heel of her hand or thumb. Before she left, she told me again that I must see a Western doctor and have whatever it was in my body removed.

A British specialist who worked out of Hong Kong and came to Shanghai once a month confirmed that what Dr. Kao had told me was true and underlined that it was 'big, irregular, and suspicious looking', as in it could be cancer. It was too deep to biopsy without removing it. Bottom line, it needed to come out, the sooner the better. I didn't want to hear it, but I had no choice.

An intense sense of guilt came over me, like I had done it to myself. A result of the stress and pressure I'd been under trying to make this impossible dream a reality. And what about those years of smoking? How stupid am I? I was so angry with myself. Funny enough, the news made me really want to smoke a cigarette...

I was scared. Really scared. I wanted my mother. I wanted to go home. What if it was cancer? Would I lose my breast? What about my career? I didn't dare say these things out loud to anyone though. Not even to Norman, who was more shaken by it than I was.

The doctor insisted that it was not safe to operate in Mainland China. He didn't trust the cleanliness of the facilities and said people often woke up from the anesthesia in the middle of surgery, which can cause traumatic nightmares that never go away. I'd have to go to Hong Kong for the operation. I couldn't afford this on so many levels. But now that we had a few weeks off before we could reopen and a reason to go to Hong Kong for the vodka company show anyways, I decided to schedule the surgery and get it over with.

The bad news kept coming. We were owed a hundred grand from our tenant at the Chelsea Hotel. He was a thirty-year-old trust fund kid with a Jesus complex, who called himself a documentary filmmaker. There was something really odd about him that I never liked personally. He was the kind of guy who wore a t-shirt with a wolf howling at the moon and tried to pretend he wasn't wearing it to be an ironic hipster. He kept saying the overdue payment was coming, but the last email Norman sent had gone unanswered.

We got a note from a neighbor at The Chelsea saying that dick-boy had trashed the house, packed his car in the middle of the night and took off. Because of him we lost our lease, our New York apartment, not to mention, a hundred grand that was still withstanding, which we could've used right about then. We were considering asking Tino's close associates to pay him a visit. The letter also said that our beloved garden had been completely ripped out. Nothing remained. The hotel was up for sale. They were starting to kick out long-term residents. With the art off the walls and people coming home to find their apartments padlocked, the future of the landmark was in troubling limbo. Everyone said that we had left just in time. Having lived there for twenty-five years, Norman was glad he wasn't there to witness the demise, but was still immensely saddened by the turn of events.

It also said that our dear mate, Arthur Weinstein, had passed away. He died of throat cancer. The news hit Norman like a ton of bricks. They were best friends, almost the same age. I think it was hearing this that made Norman urge me to go ahead and schedule the surgery and to stop worrying about the considerable expense of it. The money would come, he assured me. And worse comes to worst, I could pay the balance with one of my two well-tapped credit cards. I tried not to think about the affect it would have on my life. Besides my vanity - because, lets be real, my breasts are a major part of my showgirl image – there was the fact that I wouldn't be able to dance during the recovery period. And I couldn't even begin to fathom what it would mean if it was, god forbid, cancerous.

At the office, Norman and I were beginning to notice another problem emerge. One of the stipulations of Beth Peterson's investment was that she got to look after all the company's bookkeeping, and we trusted her to do a good job. Meanwhile, Dougie wasn't showing up to the office as frequently as he used to, but he always had an off-site meeting to attend or some other reason.

Beth insisted that we do everything one hundred percent by the book. From contracts to visas to performance licenses, 'Or else we'll go to jail', she would say. While Norman and I agreed that jail would be bad, we'd been working on this project for over two years already and understood that a lot of how business actually gets done in China has absolutely nothing to do with the rulebook. Adopting this militant philosophy was causing unwarranted payouts and scrutiny. Unnecessary problems that otherwise could have been avoided had we stuck to doing things the real Chinese way like everyone else. When we pointed out to her that people like August Helm had been running multinational businesses in Shanghai for thirty years on a tourist visa, or that none of the other clubs signed long-term contracts with their dancers, allowing them to avoid the loopholes in the Chinese labor and tax laws, she'd go stiff and unresponsive. The clear implication being that if we didn't want to do things her way, she would retract her investment, which left little room for discussion or negotiation, especially because she seemed to take any questioning of her methods personally.

In addition to the approaching Hong Kong vodka show, we picked up another high-profile gig, which was good because it meant we kept the showgirls busy and practicing while we sorted out the fallout from the sound violations. The fifth anniversary party for the five-star restaurant on the Bund, Laris, had the theme 'Vegas Comes to Hollywood'. One of the features of the party we produced for them included Reverend Benny Sideways hosting a chapel, equipped with feet outlines on the ground indicating where two people must stand to be wed. He asked the tough questions like, 'Do you promise not to get upset if you find gang-bang Latino porn on your husband's laptop?' and if he was satisfied with the answers, the newly-weds received a marriage certificate that expired at midnight. He encouraged the new couples to kiss. You can imagine the sensation it caused when Kayla and Heidi-Sue got married and kissed. The former Muslim and the former Mormon.... Just saying. There was a Keno wheel with branded prizes, an arcade-style photo-op where faces went through holes to become Elvis and Pricilla Presley, and we even had a 3-D, B-Movie theatre marquee set up over the oyster bar.

Freddy was the star of four brand new production numbers. I had barely finished making all the costumes in time for the party. That night, Brenna and Star joined Freddy on stage for 'The Coffee Song'. The girls wore colorful, neon, Carmen Miranda-style get-ups with ruffled armbands, detachable skirts, and fringe bras and bottoms that whipped back and forth over their tanned skin. I'd made the headdresses from the weightless, paper, Confucian, burn-for-the-dead fruit balanced high on their heads like Chiquita Banana.

The four men - Norman, Freddy, Rupert and Benny - performed as The Rat Pack and I'm pleased to say that they could really swing, ring-a-ding! They performed 'Style' with Norman doing quick-changes, appearing in several outlandish outfits before he finally gets it right in an Astaire-quality tuxedo, because, '*You've either got, or you haven't got Sty-le!*'

For our standout production number of the night, we performed 'Luck Be a Lady' for the first time. Freddy sang the classic song as four Dolls in red and black showgirl costumes kicked their legs out from under blown-up playing cards of the four Queens. Benny Sideways made a cameo in showgirl drag, costing Freddy to lose a straight mid-song, but then I came out as Lady Luck herself, giving him a royal flush.

After we came off stage, Josephine continued the scandalous tale she was in the middle of telling us before we went on.

"...But I still had my key, right? Which he obviously hadn't considered, and I knew she was going to be there, right? So I show myself in, and I - could - hear - them..."

She stopped and growled towards the ceiling. Brenna and I exchanged bug-eyed looks.

"So I go into the bedroom, grab the bitch by her stupid hair and throw her out the flat."

"You didn't," said Brenna.

"Oh yes I did. But wait, that's not even the best part. Well, so, she's outside- "

"Naked?" Kayla squeaked.

"Yeah. But then I took his TV and threw it out the window at her!" She smiled wickedly.

"What?" Brenna threw her head back laughing. "You are unbelievable Josephine."

"And the best part is, it was his new TV that he had just saved up to buy to replace the last one I threw out the window."

We looked at her with dropped jaws before bursting into bewildered laughter.

Showgirls. What can I say?

Before the finale, we presented the restaurant owner with a giant, tiered cake on wheels. I popped out of it as a sultry, breathless Marilyn Monroe, singing 'Happy Anni-ver-sary, to, you!' The culinary tycoon turned beet red and broke into a sweat. Last but not least, we did 'Viva Las Vegas'. Showgirls, Elvis, conga line, what more could you ask for?

After my duties were done I drank two martinis and went home to make love to my husband like there was no tomorrow.

CHAPTER 24 – Hong Kong Phooey

There was a tomorrow though. We both woke up hungover, tired and acutely aware of what was approaching. In two days we'd do one of the first burlesque shows in Hong Kong, then everyone besides me and Freddy would fly back to Shanghai and I'd have surgery. Norman couldn't leave the site or office for longer than completely necessary. The construction workers brought in to fix the soundproofing and finish the job they were supposed to have finished for the opening were bent on doing the least amount of work possible. He was always catching them in lies, saying they had done things when they hadn't. Norman figured that it took an average of three times before they actually did the right thing. It was like some kind of a game: Try to screw over the lǎowài lǎo bǎn. The kind of game people might play in hell.

Freddy had to get a new visa so he planned to stay an extra few days in Hong Kong anyways. He'd be there to look after me when I got out of the hospital, and then we'd fly back home together after I got the results.

It hadn't occurred to me that we were flying in the height of the bird flu epidemic. Once we landed in Hong Kong, we were instructed to stay in our seats as two people came on board wearing white, full body, head-to-toe astronaut suits with goggles and white masks covering the rest of their faces. They marched to the back of the plane, young children hysterical at the sight of them. They carried big guns shaped like semi-automatics that pointed directly at foreheads, red laser crosshairs that read temperatures. Anyone with a suspicious temperature was brought to the front of the plane to be examined.

When Josephine got called to the front, I thought I might hyperventilate. Selfishly, I was thinking about the fact that if one of the Dolls was pulled out at this point we'd have to re-choreograph our numbers on the spot, and I knew the client wouldn't be happy. I closed my eyes and said a quick prayer, apologizing again for not really being a believer and only calling when I was desperate. *But if you're out there, could you please not send Josephine back to Shanghai? Please?*

We all clapped when she was released and returned to her seat. I breathed a heavy sigh of relief, especially when I heard that another plane had a mandatory quarantine ordered for every passenger due to one person with a fever. They made all the passengers stay in a crappy hotel for five days while the military stood guard, no one allowed to leave.

When Norman and I went to scope out the venue with the vodka company clients, they said the event had a strong buzz and was getting a lot of attention in the local media. We had a day's worth of interviews before the show, and the guest list was a who's-who of Hong Kong celebrities and socialites. It was invigorating to hear that Chinatown was a popular topic of conversation there, too. Everyone kept asking us to open one in Hong Kong. We just might, I'd say.

After the seamless show, we posed for photos with the clients and guests, indulging in the free vodka that was practically forced down our throats. Dougie said he was approached by someone interested in hiring us for the opening of a hotel in Borneo, which was exciting. When I found myself alone at a table with Dougie, I told him that I felt like we hadn't gotten to just hang out like we used to in a long time. Then I asked him if he was okay. In a flash, he changed from being his carefree, over the top self, to a scowl, snapping, "Yeah, I'm fine, why wouldn't I be?"

"No reason babe, just making sure." I let it go, figuring that he may have had a few too many free vodkas.

The next morning in bed, Norman and I spent as long as we could lying in each other's arms. When hunger got the best of us, we hit the streets of Hong Kong. We were staying in shark fin central, where every store for blocks sold natural and unnatural concoctions, boasting of their endangered shark fins and rhino horns. At four o'clock the group congregated in the lobby. Star, Kayla, Brenna and Josephine formed a tight, protective huddle around me. They could see I was starting to get nervous about the surgery and hugged me, assuring me that everything was going to be all right. I felt really lucky that I could call these girls my friends.

The last people to show were Rupert, Dougie and Heidi-Sue. As soon as they walked out of the elevator wearing sunglasses, everyone gasped. They were severely sunburned. Lobster-red.

In his slow drawl, Freddy asked on behalf of everyone, "What the hell happened to you guys?"

Smiling like rascals when they took their sunglasses off, they had white raccoon eyes. They were painful to look at, like looking directly at the sun. When they finally managed to string a couple of words together in an order that made sense, it came out that they had stayed up all night tripping on acid. At some point they found the beach and lost their sunscreen, from the looks of things.

Norman and I kissed goodbye, and then they were gone. Freddy put his arm around me.

"Welcome to life kid... Let's get a beer!"

It only took a few sips before I realized that it was probably a good thing Freddy was the one staying with me. If Norman was there we would both be worried. This way I felt compelled to keep my composure and remain stable company for Freddy's sake. Considering the circumstances, we actually had a pretty good time. We shared stories about first loves, various scars we'd acquired over the years, and what life was like growing up. I prodded him to say which showgirl he fancied the most.

"You mean, besides you?" he said looking at his beer, making me laugh. Always a charmer that one.

"Yes Freddy, besides me," I blushed.

"Well, I mean, they're all cute girls," he said, trying to back out of answering the question.

"Freddy, come on, you have to pick one!"

"Alright," he said seriously, like it was top secret, classified information. He even looked over both shoulders as if checking to make sure his soon-to-be-ex-wife wasn't going to pop out of a corner.

Finally, he leaned in and whispered, "Star."

"I knew it, I knew it! I could see it when you kissed at the end of 'Shanghai Lil'. So what are you waiting for, you going to give it a go or what?"

"She has a boyfriend... Why? Do you think she might...? Nah, we work together, it wouldn't be right. Anyways, I feel very protective over you girls. We've got a good thing going here, you know? I wouldn't want to chance ruining that."

When I woke up from the surgery he was holding my hand, tears in his eyes. He stayed with me as I received the news that the tumor was, thankfully, found to be benign. He even argued on my behalf when the bill came to eight hundred HKD more than they had quoted me before the operation.

While we were away our beloved heritage building had been painted beige by the local government. Beige! Nevermind that in our contract it specifically stated that the facade of the building could not be altered in any way, shape or form because of its heritage status. And it wasn't just our building either. Every building on the whole damn block got the brush, it was a citywide makeover in preparation for the World Expo, and there was nothing anyone could do about it. But that was the least of our concerns.

When Norman returned to the club, Harley's team was working at a snail's pace. One guy would paint the same small patch of wall over and over again, while a second guy stood next to him staring into space, holding his paint bucket. When Norman got furious over their lousy work ethic, he confronted the onsite supervisor. The supervisor informed him through Goldfish that the crew wanted Harley to raise their pay by three cents an hour, and until Harley granted them this, they'd continue to work in this fashion.

Norman went up to a guy who had been painting the same spot for ten minutes. He took the bucket from his friend and went to town, showing them how it was supposed to be done. After he covered half the wall, satisfied that he had demonstrated his point, he turned around. All the workers had stopped what they were doing and formed a crowd, watching him. Norman presented his wall with a smile, then shooed the workers off to get back to work. No one moved. Goldfish whispered to him that he could not do that, for now the workers had lost face.

Face is a popular topic of speculation amongst expats. The Chinese will deny its very existence, but that practically underlines the concept. I'd describe face as how one is seen to be seen. For instance, the whole obsession with Western labels, like Burberry and Louis Vuitton. If you are seen wearing these labels that means you can afford luxury Western goods, and being perceived as rich gives someone face. It's a simple enough concept, one that we Westerners can easily relate to. It's in losing face that things get tricky, and is not to be underestimated.

I had my own theories about face, something one develops to hold your own across dinner tables in the never-ending attempts by expats to make sense out of Chinese behavior. My theory is that it has a lot to do with China's past, with the Cultural Revolution. The rest of the world watched that shit go down: The mass genocide, famine, the inhumanity of it all. It's very recent history. In retrospect, it's clear that it was a huge loss of face for Chinese people as a whole.

You get some people who go on about China being the oldest culture in the world. But to anyone who's spent time here, its pretty obvious that 'Traditional Chinese Culture' is about as relevant to modern China as the Red Indians are to Manhattan. The culture is really only twenty-odd years old. Mao erased everything before that with the Revolution. And to this day, there has never been any direct or indirect acknowledgement of the devastation of any of it by the people, press or government. Chairman Mao is still on their currency, for heck's sake. No one can even mention the Cultural Revolution. Everyone is just supposed to pretend it never happened. Generations of a whole society living with an unspeakable, unreconciled shadow of shame.

How this affects modern business dealings, where face and the loss of face is so important, is that it has bred generations of people who are unwilling to take personal responsibility for anything that could potentially make them look bad. Someone messes up, it's never his or her fault. If it was, that would be a loss of face, and employees will quit before admitting or accepting that they haven't done something right or to standard. A perceived loss of face, especially to a foreigner, can result in multi-million dollar deals down the drain, contracts declared void, and revenge. It can mean the end of everything, right then and there.

Norman told Goldfish that he didn't care and that he didn't give two shits about whether or not the workers lost face.

"They aren't doing their job. I'm the one paying them. They should get it right! So what? I can't work on my own club? You're telling me that they're telling me that I can't pick up a paintbrush in my own club when no one else can get it right? I told this guy three times what I wanted him to do, and three times he fucked it up, and I'm just supposed to watch this stupidity? Fine. Fuck it. Fuck it all to hell!"

He had to go outside before he killed someone. The bullshit was getting to him. He called Harley and told him about the lazy workers, and asked him to please get a hold of his men because time was running out. He was polite with Harley though. Always. By now we had sussed out that Harley was a dangerously well-connected thug, make no mistake about that. And Norman was well aware of just how delicate the feelings of his insecure tribe were. So he controlled himself, spoke clearly and respectfully, and in return Harley assured him that he'd take care of the problem.

PART 3:

YEAR OF THE SHOWGIRL

CHAPTER 25 – Miss Chinatown

And we were back, reopening on Halloween with the most sensational party in town. While we were closed, the word spread about Chinatown. All the various rumors of why we had been shutdown only made everyone want to come and experience our forbidden pleasure palace more.

Norman and I started getting requests for interviews from prestigious papers and magazines, both local and international. We had color spreads and feature articles in Newsweek, Australia's Financial Review, The Wall Street Journal and Conde Nast Traveler, positioning Gosney & Kallman as the 'Dynamic duo of nightlife', set to secure Shanghai once again as 'The Paris of the East'. During these interviews we made sure not to disclose anything other than complete support for The Party and the unique Chinese business practices. We were always quoted saying things like, 'We believe China is the future' and 'We are here to learn' in order to assure our good standing with the government.

My recovery from surgery wasn't as bad as I anticipated and soon enough, I was ready to go again. Performing four nights a week and rehearsing during the days, our repertoire of original, saucy, new-vaudeville material expanded weekly. I was still trying to find my balance between being a fulltime showgirl, director, owner, friend, wife, lover... Overnight it became pretty full-on. I never worked so hard in my life. But I still felt like I had a lot to prove, even if it was just to myself. I wanted to prove that I could handle all the pressures and stress that came my way, because at the end of the day, I got to stand up there on that stage, my stage, and do what I loved to do. I had the best job in the world and I was living the dream. It doesn't get much better than that.

It was ten o'clock on a Friday night and Chinatown was starting to heat up. Our award-winning bar staff were shaking cocktails, as the glamorous showgirls strutted around saying hello to their favorite customers.

Tonight's audience were typical for a Friday night: A large number of single expats, usually in groups, spending their generous salaries on the good life, a nice showing of couples who understood this was the best night out in town, and a very healthy proportion of tourists, as we were now the crown jewel of the retro, Shanghai-in-its-heyday circuit. The early crowd enjoyed fine dining while listening to the solid four-piece jazz combo playing everything from Big Band Swing to Bebop to Boogaloo, while Freddy, Kayla and Benny took turns singing along. Then there was the after dinner crowd of regulars and cool expats showing off their city to visitors, and we'd get another wave of hard-partiers showing up after midnight. We received a lot of emails from tourists who were just passing through the city, thanking us for the best night they've ever had at a nightclub. One article tried to sum it up by saying, 'If Shanghai has a heart, Chinatown is that heart'.

On Wednesday and Thursday nights we found that our audiences were largely local businessmen and women, so I'd put up a lot of Chinese-centric acts. Generally though, the local reaction was hard to figure. The Chinese women in the audience often didn't drink and barely clapped. It was tough to say what kind of impression we made on them. Others recorded us on cellphone cameras. I wanted to shake these people and say, 'We're live - right here in front of you! Why are you watching us through the one inch monitor of your phone?'

I watched Norman working the room in his inimitable style. After years of emceeing, he had now taken the main floor as his personal stage. Describing himself as 'A million dollar doorman', he made a point to greet and shake hands with every customer upon arrival, and then thanked them each for coming on their way out.

"The idea is to have 3,000 best friends," he told me. "If a punter can say they know the owner, they'll keep coming back."

He was able to pull off the masterful trick of visiting with every table of revelers just long enough to make them feel like the coolest table in the house, and then politely extricate himself on 'showbiz duties', as to not get stuck into conversation. I could tell that at times it was difficult for him not to leap up on stage, as he is such an incorrigible show-off, but no one else can host a room the way he does.

In fifteen minutes we would start our third big block of show for the night. In my head, I ran through a checklist. I was always running backstage to check in with the cast. They were now a professional, eye-popping troupe that could compete anywhere in the world, but things still got forgotten in the dressing room, some of the costume changes had to be pre-set, props pre-positioned, egos stroked... We had been worried that we weren't going to find the talent we needed in Shanghai, but the lengthy period it had taken to open had actually turned out to be an advantage in that respect, as I got to mold the unlikely and disparate group into one of the best ensemble casts I'd ever worked with. We weren't doing straight-ahead burlesque either. There were elements of burlesque, cabaret and vaudeville, but it was more like 1940's showbiz meets the 21st century, with Chinese elements and gags running throughout. Every night we were breaking new ground, doing entertainment unlike any other in the world, and it felt great.

Rupert had really found his stride and was doing a smashing job emceeing, winding the crowd up when necessary, presenting the smaller and solo acts with loving aplomb, and often doing a piece himself, sometimes in Mandarin. On Saturday nights he hosted our Best Dressed Competition. It became so popular that people came competitively dressed to win. The winner got to sit center stage while the showgirls sang and danced in a production number. The showgirl who nominated the winner, having plucked them from the audience pool, gave the victor some extra special attention, tickling them with a feather or giving them a lap dance. Let's just say that some girls were less shy than others.

Tonight in the Absinthe Room, we were expecting a party of eight high-rollers, courtesy of Lufthansa Airlines who permanently reserved the box for their first-class customers. David Lynch's film crew occupied the Red Rum Room, and the Champagne Room was hosting a rowdy hen party. We had two groups of Chinese big shots in two separate rooms that were competitively trying to outspend each other on high-priced bottles of our finest whiskey. One of the groups was already looking a bit worse for wear though. The curtains were closed in the Lover's Box, but inside was just a group of rich, young local guys playing dice games, which always made me wonder why they came to a place like ours in the first place. The nouveau rich Chinese recognized and were attracted to the new and hip, but it's like they hadn't quite figured out how to join in yet.

On the main floor, the rear-wall banquets under the mezzanine facing the stage, were filling up with the gonna-be-here-all-night regulars. In front of those, over twenty small tables, very romantic in a Weimar-style, waited for couples, small gatherings, and stray souls who we would try to put together with other solos, often to great effect. We knew of at least two couples so far who had met on our main floor. I watched a couple take a table, French or German my guess. The guy had taken the trouble to dress in a three-piece suit, looking suave, and his girl was approvingly licking her lips after tasting her Virginia Slim, a cocktail named after me. From their body language and gestures I could tell that they were just 'discovering' Chinatown and having a brilliant second or third date.

I made sure to let our regulars know that Kayla would be debuting her new 'Teach Me Tiger' burlesque

221

act, which was too hot for the main stage, in our third floor VIP bar during our secret, late-night, afterhours party.

In between the acts, The Acid Ponies veejayed projected video mixes onto the stage, using elements of Busby Berkeley, German Expressionist cinema, Bettie Page bondage films, Anna May Wong, Esther Williams, Marilyn Monroe, and nightclub scenes from film noirs, all cunningly entwined and edited to make something entirely new. I had to watch what we showed though. Norman once thought it would be fun to show the trailer for the film *Freaks*. While much revered in collector's circles, the film is extremely weird and off the wall to the uninitiated. I ran to the tech booth, demanding they turn it off immediately, but it was too late, we had already offended some tables who decided to leave. We wouldn't be showing that film again anytime soon.

Next up was our 'King Kong' number, a three-part scorcher. It involved the showgirls onstage dressed as Amazons in tiny leopard bikinis with spears and shields. They kidnap Freddy and tie him up. I enter in a huge gorilla costume, paraded through the crowd by Norman, until I break my chains, giving some of the tipsy girls in the audience a true fright. Then onstage, the showgirls strip me out of the ape suit to reveal my showgirl-shape in a nude, sparkling rhinestone bra and g-string, with black tribal, tattooed tights. I tease Freddy while the showgirls take his shirt off, only to be interrupted by Rupert dressed as Superman, there to save the day.

The ending references an earlier sequence from the beginning of the show when Star and Benny give Rupert a Chinese name. He is told the name means

'Superman', when in fact it means 'Little Penis', so when Rupert rushes the stage declaring, 'Wǒ jiào Xiǎo dì dì!' or 'I am Little Penis!' the Chinese speakers in our audience fall out of their seats laughing. We were definitely doing something right, because evenings like these felt like magic, onstage and off.

After the long nights, Norman and I sat around our kitchen table discussing the show, the audience, gossiping about the latest hook-ups or fights within the dramatic family we had created, which now extended to our regular. Our creative juices would be flowing, and that was when we came up with some of our best ideas for acts, props and burlesques. By the time we'd go to bed, the sun would be coming up. We'd pull the shades, sleep until noon, and then wake up and do it all again.

Sundays the Ayi would wake us up at noon and we'd treat ourselves to an American style brunch at Keven's on Hengshan Lu, before hitting the DVD store, and returning back to our love nest. If we were lucky, we got to have Monday off as well, to go to the gym and create some semblance of a normal life.

When we did see our way clear to go out for dinner or drinks, we were now treated like local heroes. Maître 'ds would send over bottles of champagne, or the chef would send out special dishes and make sure we never saw a bill. It wasn't just us who couldn't believe we pulled off the miracle of Chinatown. Many of the more perceptive expats understood what a difficult challenge it had been, and gave us immense respect for seeing it through. When I went out with the showgirls we never paid for drinks, and fans would fawn over their favorite dancer, detailing their favorite parts of each act. Norman and I were even getting recognized and stopped in the streets. Almost weekly the guy at our local newsstand would be waiting to show us our latest magazine features, or me on the cover of Elite, or our spreads in GQ, Vogue, Harper's Bazaar and DestinAsia. Even Beijing's own China Daily gave us a two-page, center spread with the best government approved sound bite we could have asked for, declaring, 'Every City Needs a Chinatown'.

CHAPTER 26 – Pervert Party

"If the police show up tonight, and for some reason they insist on coming in, and I can't stop them, then I'll hit the alarm," Beth told the cast in the boy's dressing room as we all got ready for a risqué Pervert Party.

"So you'll hear 'Twinkle Twinkle Little Star' or 'Mary Had a Little Lamb'. And if you do, I'm just going to say this once so it's clear. Put clothes on...." The boys snickered. "Put your clothes on, and hold tight. Logan, I think you're the only one this applies to now because I don't have your paperwork yet. You'll need to go through the trapdoor and exit through the tunnel under the stage like we talked about, okay? And don't come back until one of us calls you. So keep your phone on you just in case. Capiche?"

Logan was our new stage manager. A cute, short Jewish guy about my age from Long Island, with an afro of brown, kinky hair. He became my right-hand man. I never had to tell him anything twice, and he usually did things before I asked him anyways. A teacher in real life, he was too smart for the job, but I wasn't about to tell him that.

Beth handed out the latest calendar of upcoming events. The club was the most popular spot in town, everyone wanted to have their parties at Chinatown. We had the launch for Time Out Shanghai, a Dolce & Gabbana party, a wrap party for the David Lynch-Dior commercial, a Karl Lagerfeld event, and a Tiffany's party in Hong Kong. Also, our upcoming show in Borneo, Malaysia for the opening of The Pullman Kuching Hotel. And for all those events there were costumes to be made, acts to be choreographed, rehearsals... Busy times.

"Any questions?" Beth asked, wrapping up the meeting. Star, dressed in a sexy nurse's uniform, raised her hand.

"I don't know the 'Twinkle Little Star' or the 'Mary'...? What's that?"

In unison, the cast broke out into a musical rendition of the classic nursery rhymes. The boys started bopping in three-part harmony, with the girls singing back-up. Freddy got down on one knee to personally serenade Star. He looked sexy in his costume for the evening: An unzipped jumpsuit and aviators, as if he'd been under cars changing oil all day. Then we went into rounds of 'Mary Had a Little Lamb'. You could tell it was the last show on a Saturday night because we were all getting punchy, over-confident and borderline menacing. We were like a wolf pack of theatre geeks. You wouldn't want to get in our way. We might start using awkward alliteration or blow glitter in your face, or spontaneously start taking our clothes off at inappropriate times.

In my long, red wig, shiny black police hat, booty shorts, and thigh-high black bondage boots,

Kayla yanked the strings of my zebra corset until I couldn't breathe.

Since being a showgirl fulltime, I was finding that I had no interest in dressing up like I used to just for fun. It felt too much like work. Off the clock, I preferred instead to bury myself in cozy comfort, dressing like a tomboy with no make-up whatsoever. I think it's easy for some people to have the wrong impression of showgirls, burlesque artists and strippers. People assume that if someone is seductive and provocative onstage, that they're that way in real life. We're all sex-crazed maniacs out to steal other people's boyfriends and husbands. I thought that too before I knew better, which is really funny because, honestly, it couldn't be further from the truth. Dressing up sexy and exposing yourself to strangers takes something out of your sex life. Expectations about you change, and what you want changes too.

That's one advantage to having a lover in the business. Most showgirls I know prefer to have a steady lover, male or female, who's supportive and understands that there's a difference between what someone does for a living and who they really are, like any other job.

It's a challenge to feel sexy when you're exhausted though. But there I was, dressed in showgirl uniform, ready for the final show of the day. It had already been a long one with a photo shoot, an interview with The Guardian, rehearsals for a new Chinese sketch comedy act, an off-site show for the Tatler Magazine Ball, a regular show for three birthday parties, and still to come, the sleazy Pervert Party. Then my weekend would finally begin.

My dinner arrived from the kitchen. I sat shoving a duck and foie gras hot dog down my throat. I'd been eating pre-prepared food from the club for almost every meal. Our kitchen was generating a revenue stream that we hadn't foreseen. When Norman originally talked to Dougie about selling 'hundred kwai hotdogs', it was a figurative reference to ten-dollar hotdogs that bars in New York serve in order to qualify for a coveted Tavern License. Dougie took him literally though, resulting in our best selling, specialty items: Gourmet hot-dogs. The twelve-inch Big Frankie was the most popular. We also had a girl push around a dessert cart featuring delicious chocolate treats, a rarity in Shanghai.

The food wasn't the healthiest however. I wasn't sure how I was staying slim. I guess I burned more calories dancing around on stage every night than I realized. The other showgirls were constantly going on diets, eating only kiwis or pineapples, or drinking maple syrup. I was on the high-stress, lack of sun and sleep diet. It seemed to be working, but I wouldn't recommend it.

"I highly doubt that the Illuminati had anything to do with Michael Jackson's death, Benny," Rupert said in his formal Welsh Guards Officer's uniform.

"No, it's true, swear to God," Benny defended. "And Gene Simmons was in on it."

"Gene Simmons? Why do you have to bring Kiss into it? Isn't anything sacred anymore?"

"Think what you want man, but I know it's true. You know how I know? At Michael's funeral right, Gene was seen to stick his tongue out."

Logan and I exchanged looks. It was especially funny because Benny was sat there in costume, dressed as a sex slave with a ball gag and leash around his neck, ready for the 'Pervert Parade'. It was hard not to laugh in his face about one conspiracy theory or another sometimes, bless him. He told me the other day that when he was nineteen he legally changed his name to Cloud Vegas. And he had already given me his resignation for 2012, because, you know, that's when the world was going to end. Otherwise, he was a really sweet and talented, lovable guy. What amused me though, was just how popular he was with the local ladies. They fought over him, literally.

I ditched the guy's dressing room for the girl's. Opening the door, there was something behind it. It was Heidi-Sue's cute, freckle-faced kid playing his handheld video game. He had a grimace on his little face, as if being in a showgirl's dressing room was the last place in the world he wanted to be. If only he knew... I took my place at the vanity next to Heidi-Sue and asked her if her Ayi was coming to pick him up.

"I'm a mother, Amelia. I couldn't get a babysitter, so I had no choice. He's here, okay?" she snapped adjusting her white, curly, Marie Antoinette wig.

"Sorry, I didn't mean it like that, I was just asking."

Every time I attempted to talk to her these days, this was the attitude I got. Since we found out that what Kayla said was true, about how she went behind our backs after we turned down her costume proposal, and how she manipulated Beth into approving it, you could say there was tension between us. When I confronted her about it, I gave her a chance to explain. For a girl who never stopped talking, and never stopped talking about herself for that matter, words escaped her. She stammered and muttered. Said something about Beth saying it was fine.

I reminded her that Beth wasn't her boss. I was. And while I liked her as a showgirl, to go behind me and Norman's back like that after we said no was most unprofessional, and really not cool on any level. And if she ever double-crossed one of us again, I wouldn't hesitate to replace her. I would've fired her right then and there, but Beth's been hesitant to fire anyone since that local thieving waitress sued us. When it became apparent that Heidi-Sue wasn't going to own up or apologize, I added that she had disappointed me as a friend too. Maybe I shouldn't have said that, because that's when she turned on me. For the sake of the others, I'd gone out of my way to try to keep things civil. I took lots of deep breaths and tried my damnedest to just ignore her and not let her get to me. At least onstage she was still performing well.

"Oh my god, I am so tired!" Kayla exclaimed. Her costume for the evening was… Well, practically nothing. I swear, that girl's allergic to clothes. Wearing lacey, light pink panties and a ruffled bra with black stockings and a garter belt, she looked about fifteen. I pitied her poor Muslim father for ever attempting to contain her. A goal I had in life was to persuade her not to get pregnant for a few more years. She was young, gorgeous, and one of the most talented people I'd ever met, but her culture and upbringing dictated that she must fall in love and start popping out babies as soon as possible, and she was on the prowl for Mister Right.

"So you know I went home with model-boy last night-" she started.

"You mean coke-addict, player boy?" Josephine teased.

"Yeah, him." Kayla missed the joke. "Well, he was so high on whiskey and cocaine that he couldn't even screw me. Can you believe it? He's a limp dick! I am… shocked."

The girls started to discuss the details. Size, length, thickness, etc. Full disclosure. No one is safe in the girl's dressing room.

"Hey, I'm about to head to the kitchen and see if they'll let me have a brownie," I stated. "Can I bring him?" I asked Heidi-Sue.

The kid looked up from his game, bobbing his head up and down, pleading to go. She said it was okay.

"Come on then" I said, and he followed me like a shadow. I wondered what he must think of me in this ridiculous dominatrix costume. In the kitchen I introduced him to our chef and Ayi, who broke out the brownies for him on my request. Ayi said she would be happy to look after him and keep him occupied. He spoke to her in fluent Chinese, better than I spoke. Later, when I went in to check on him, the little man was stood on a stool in an apron in front of the sink.

"I've been promoted to dishwasher!" he said gleefully, showing me his missing front tooth as he grinned.

I went out to the front of the house to see if we'd have room to do the parade through the audience. The place was so packed, there was no way. We would have to do it onstage. For the night's event we made a deejay booth on the band platform for the Acid Ponies, and took all the tables and chairs out, so it was just a dance floor. Pushing through the crowd to the front door, I slid the screen of the Judas hole to have a peek outside. The street was rammed, two hundred or more people in fancy dress stretching down the road. Norman was organizing them into a line with his cane like a cattle prod. He was going Studio 54 on them, only letting in the people he wanted to: The best dressed girls, people he knew, the ones who slipped him wads of bills or other forms of payment.

Before we started the parade, the girls were in a twitter. The costume was affecting my personality and I was Dom-ing everyone into places when I realized Heidi-Sue was nowhere to be found.

"Has anyone seen Heidi-Sue?" I sighed.

The girls broke out into devilish giggles. There was some kind of joke going on… Was it on me?

"She's in The Lov-er's Box," Brenna sang teasingly. I stuck my head through the curtain to see if I could see her, but the audience took this as a sign the show was about to begin and started whooping. The curtains in the Lover's Box were closed, but moving from the inside. Over the walkie-talkie I had Claude in the tech booth go and fetch her. A few minutes later she appeared in the wings where we were waiting for her to begin. After the parade, a fight broke out between Heidi-Sue and Kayla. Apparently, the guy she had been up there with was one of Kayla's exes, and Kayla had only introduced them an hour earlier.

Luckily, they made a truce before the finale, which was a very special one-off number that really brought the house down. Red towels covered the stage and there was a big silver bowl full of baby oil. Need I say more?

Brenna was the first showgirl out in her little black bikini, black bob wig and high heels. She laid herself down across the towels and sensuously raised one of her perfectly toned legs up in the air. With her fingertips, she slowly rubbed a shiny streak of oil down her calf and then her thigh, making coy eyes at the audience the whole time. Under the moody yellow light, we joined her one by one, each of us dressed identical. While the Acid Pony Club spun a sultry beat, we rubbed oil all over each other's bodies, slowly traveling up and down, getting in between legs with hands and faces, grabbing one another close, bending over, rubbing oil over stomachs and breasts and shoulders and hips and asses. At the climax we moved into position, crotch to ass, hands clutching pelvises, and we snapped our heads to face the audience at the same time.

The curtains closed. It took everyone in the building a few seconds to catch their breath.

"Oh. My. God. That was so-o-o hot!" Kayla squealed with joy.

"That wasn't so bad, was it?" I asked with a saucy smile, looking down at my hard, perky nipples.

"Wow," Josephine said, her eyes wide. She looked dumbfounded.

"That was better than sex," said Brenna coolly.

"You all right?" I asked Star, hoping I hadn't completely corrupted her.

She took a moment to reflect and then said, "I want to do again!"

Piling into the boy's dressing room we started to towel off, floating and giggling, ecstatic from whatever sex-magic just took place.

Rupert took one look at us and burst, "Genius! Pure genius. I don't think there is a man or woman in this building without a huge throbbing hard-on right now. That's probably instigated orgies in all the booths, happening as we speak."

Freddy and Logan were speechless, but the unstoppable grins spoke volumes.

Freddy finally turned to the boys and said, "Do we have the best job in the world, or what?"

That was us done! The cast rushed to join the party and get drunk. Heidi-Sue and Kayla did more than make up that night, they made out in the Juliet balcony for all to see. I opted to stand guard backstage, keeping civilians from doing drugs or having sex in our private toilet. I'd tell them that the backstage toilet was strictly for cast members to do drugs and have sex in. Freddy had the same idea, to hide out, as well as a bottle of whiskey.

"Let's toast it up, Freddy. We freakin' deserve it."

"You alright there?" he asked me in his Southern drawl. I gave him a look, one that he recognized. "Want to talk about it?" I shook my head. Pouring us each a glass, we held them in the air.

"What are we drinking to?" he asked.

"The good old days? 'Cause *these* are the good old days, am I right?" I smiled at him and we clinked glasses.

"No, seriously," he said, "To you, my dear. You're the one who makes this all work. We couldn't do it without you." My bottom lip quivered. Coming from him that meant a lot.

CHAPTER 27 – Revenge of the Goldfish

"Do you mind if we take a quick break please?" I said to the Chinese film crew who'd been following me around all week. When they asked if they could make a documentary about my work and Chinatown, I was truly honored, but having an amateur film crew in my face, following my every move and recording my every word had started to take a toll on my patience and nerves. My face hurt from smiling so much. The worst was when I'd say something or react to something naturally, and then they'd say, 'Oh wait, I didn't get that, can you do it again?', followed by, 'And this time, can you repeat that but look into the camera'. I had a feeling there was going to be a lot of shots of me looking directly into the camera with grated teeth, annoyed eyes, and fake smiles.

They agreed to leave me alone for a little while. I maneuvered my way through the Friday night audience, moving as unobtrusively as possible for a six-foot-tall-in-heels showgirl with a huge, red feathery headdress. I had a cigarette-girl tray around my neck as a portable store selling Freddy's CDs, my Miss Amelia

Showgirl Action Figures and DVDs, and pasties I'd made. 'Hi there,' I'd say, flirting with the customers. 'Can I interest you in taking home a souvenir from this fabulous evening? Perhaps a pair of nipple tassels for later? They come ready to wear, with double-sided tape, and I guarantee that if you buy a pair of pasties, that tonight when you go home, you will get laid, I guarantee it.' That line always worked.

Everyone assumed that because the club was hopping, and we were crowded every weekend, that we must've been rolling in it. But that wasn't strictly true. While business was great, we still hadn't recovered fully from our pre-opening debt. Soon enough though, I knew we'd be out of the red, earning real wages and not worrying about how we were going to pay our rent every month. 'The future's so bright we need sunglasses', Norman would say. A year from that point we hoped to be opening other Chinatowns around the country. Maybe Beijing, Hong Kong, Macau, or 2nd tier cities like Guangzhou or Hangzhou. That was when we would start to make the real money, money you could take back home.

I looked up at the Champagne Room to see Remco Bredenberg, Harley Zhou and Norman watching Heidi-Sue's baking burlesque, talking intently into each other's ears. Because Harley had been difficult lately, trying to push forward the repayment agreement, Remco thought it would be a good idea to bring him to the club, so he could see how popular we were, to reassure him that the money we owed him would be repaid and in the timeframe agreed upon. Remco was not my favorite person at the moment though, due to what happened with Goldfish earlier that week. It was pretty bad.

Goldfish, the Chinese liaison between us and the government departments who had been given to us and recommended by Remco, ripped us off for the equivalent of thirty grand USD! Yup. Thirty freaking G's. How could that happen? Beth relayed the story without any sense of responsibility for letting thirty grand disappear from our accounts, out from under our noses. She told us that Goldfish came into her office and said her that she needed another ten thousand towards performance licenses. Bringing up the file on these payments, Beth's records showed that we'd already paid the fees in full, as well as a large sum off the books in bribes. Suspicious, Beth asked her for the invoice, but Goldfish just kept saying over and over that another ten grand was required and pretended not to hear or understand Beth's questions. Beth asked her to take a seat and rang up someone she knew at the Cultural Department. While she was on the phone, Goldfish walked out of the office. The woman on the phone at the department told Beth that they had received the full payment from our company months ago, and there was no withstanding balance. Beth said that our records reflected that we had paid more than the number mentioned, but the woman told her she must be mistaken.

Beth hung up the phone and called for Goldfish.

"Goldfish just left," said one of the girls in the downstairs office.

Beth tried her cellphone. It was turned off. That's when it dawned on her. Goldfish had pocketed the unaccounted for thirty grand and we would probably never see her or the money again. Thirty grand! All along we'd treated Goldfish as an equal, a professional, a friend, a respected member of our team. We trusted her, and I never in a million years would have pinned her as the type to do something that blatantly criminal.

When we told Remco about it he basically smirked and called it the price of doing business in China. No indication of irony or outrage, or acknowledgement of any responsibility he might have because she came to us through him, on his recommendation. When we brought up the question of taking legal action against her, he advised us to leave it alone.

"You can't forget her position within the company," he said. "Her connections make her very powerful. If you pursue her, she might be tempted to use her connections. She is capable of doing a lot of damage. Much more than thirty grand's worth."

So we were just expected to suck it up and keep smiling for the cameras and giving interviews that said how great it was working in China. It felt like we were constantly banging our heads against a brick wall trying to do the right thing to have a healthy business in China. Between Goldfish and the waitress and Harley Zhou, we had to wonder who we could trust? And with the ever more apparent realization that, while Remco was ethnically European, he was really Chinese in thought and action, we were beginning to wonder whose team he was really playing for. Working as hard as we could everyday to make Chinatown the success we knew it could be, these betrayals felt like giant, deeply upsetting setbacks.

And it didn't help that Dougie seemed to have dropped out of the business all together. Distributers and investors he procured had been asking us where he was, and we had to make up excuses to cover for him. The truth was, we'd been asking ourselves the same question. What the hell happened to Dougie? He had a key role in the company, and his failure to cover his responsibilities, or even hand them over if he wasn't going to follow through on them, meant several important balls were getting dropped, with a domino effect of loose ends and missed opportunities.

One night Beth came in during a rehearsal with a splotchy, red-stained face. She'd been crying. She tried to cover it up with make-up, but it just made it worse. In a dark, quiet corner in the wings backstage, she reported to us dryly that Dougie had gotten a girl pregnant. The mother-to-be was a rich local girl whom he'd been seeing for several weeks.

In Shanghai, it's not unheard of for some local girls to purposefully get pregnant by foreign guys, not just for the possible financial benefits, but also the status that a mixed-race baby can bring. I'm not saying that was necessarily true in this case, but I'd heard a lot of stories about girls lying about being on the pill so they can get pregnant, then trap the father into marriage. It didn't explain Dougie's absence at work though, as you would think that a guy expecting a baby might need a job. It did explain however, some things about his erratic behavior. We assumed he must have gone off his meds to get it up for his Shanghainese princess. The Chinese believe Shanghainese girls are the most beautiful women in the world. Generally, they're expected to shop and look beautiful, while the men are supposed to work and take care of them.

We tried to reach out to him, offering our congratulations. He told us that he was coming back to work, but he never did. Just completely flaked out and let us down big-time, leaving us to take up the slack.

My horoscope had been right.

Slipping my cigarette-girl tray behind the service bar on the second floor, I climbed up the ladder to the tech booth. The Acid Ponies had covered their booth in French porn, but Brenna and Kayla snuck up there with black magic markers and drew fart clouds coming out of the naked butts. The guys were still planning their revenge. I'd started to come up there a few times a night to take refuge. It was an oasis away from the drama of backstage life, and the Ponies were always super chill and laid back.

"You look like you could use a beer," Claude said as he popped a bottle cap.

"Haha! How could you tell?" I laughed, taking a long swig. I also liked it up there because I could walkie-talkie with Logan backstage, so I was removed but not absent.

The Gazeeka Box was up. The highlight of a Friday night show, The Gazeeka Box was possibly the best act I'd ever come up with. Inspired by an obscure reference in the burlesque classic, *The Night They Raided Minsky's*, it's an audience participation act where we bring three people to the stage and ask them to imagine their fantasy lover. After each victim is forced to do a silly dance, patting heads and rubbing tummies, chanting 'Gazeeka, gazeeka, gazeeka', the magic Gazeeka Box door flies open, and their fantasy lover, played either for real or for laughs, steps forth. The best part about the act was that we could constantly switch it up, keeping even our regulars guessing who, or what, would come out next.

"Umm... Amelia? Are you there? Over," Logan's voice came through the handheld box.

"I'm here. Over."

"Umm... something's come up. Rupert's planned something with a civilian for the third Gazeeka Box entrance. Over."

"Umm... What has Rupert planned? Over."

Claude and I looked at each other. Rupert could be a bit of a loose cannon. I never knew if I was going to get playful, loveable Rupert or Nazi drill sergeant Rupert, and lately he'd been doing as he pleased, asking permission later.

"He says you'll see, but you'll like it. Over."

"I better like it. Or else," I said. "Over."

Rupert was on stage opening up the door for the second time. Brenna came on as a Catholic schoolgirl in pigtails with a lollypop. The audience hooted. Then Star came out in the same costume and they held hands, taking the lucky civilian offstage between them.

"Not one, but two, count 'em, two naughty schoolgirls," Rupert bawdily proclaimed.

The third and final contestant was a skinny, well put together local girl dressed in a flapper costume. When the door opened to the Gazeeka Box, a guy I'd never seen before in a suit with no tie and shaggy hair falling in his eyes, emerged from the box, instead of Benny Sideways.

"What...?" Claude whispered, as we both stood up to peer down from the tech booth.

On stage the guy got down on one knee, took the microphone and said, "Cathie, will you marry me?"

"Oh my gosh," I put a hand to my mouth and got tears in my eyes.

We all waited with baited breath. The showgirls stuck their heads out from behind the curtain. The girl couldn't believe it as the guy presented her with a ring. She was laughing and crying, along with the whole audience. Rupert finally held the microphone up to her mouth for an enthusiastic "Yes, Yes, I say yes!"

There wasn't a dry eye in the house. I even caught Claude choking it back. On a whim, I leaned over and kissed him on the cheek, before I climbed back down the ladder. I barged into the Champagne Room. Harley, smoking a cigarette, and Remco, with his arm around a young local girl who was not his wife, turned to see me as I came in and wrapped myself around Norman to enjoy the touching moment with him. It was an amazing feeling to be a part of that, to be the facilitators in a way of that special moment. He grabbed me close and kissed me. For a few seconds, time stood still. In the warm home of Norman's arms, life was simple again.

CHAPTER 28 – Black Burka Burlesque

We took the show on the road, out to the North West coast of Borneo, in Malaysia, to perform for the opening of the five-star Pullman Hotel. It's in the capital of Sarawak, Kuching, the City of Cats. Although we eagerly accepted the invitation to the tropical island, tanning lotion in hand, I had to wonder if there was some kind of a mix up. We specialize in sexy cabaret, vaudeville and burlesque entertainment, and Malaysia is of course, a Muslim country. To prepare our show for the occasion, I was given several rules to follow:

1. **No Skin** - No legs, thighs, midriffs, arms, shoulders, and definitely no breasts or bottoms. Nothing that looks like skin or could be mistaken for skin. Nothing nude, period. Faces were acceptable. Gee, thanks...

2. **No Contours** - No round edges of boobs or bums. That might prove over-stimulating for the conservatives in the audience.

3.   **No Stripping, Nudity, or Licentious Behavior** - Considering that most of our acts featured stripping, nudity, and licentious behavior, I had my hands full figuring out how to make this show Sarawak-ready.

On my days off, I raced around town by bike, from Yue Gardens to Qipau Lu, where all the cheapest clothing was sold. I bought tons of feather boas, tights in various colors, long gloves, and sparkling tube tops to cover midriffs. At home I constructed giant, jeweled necklaces to hide chests and made feather shoulder pieces. The day before the big show we had to do a costume parade for the perusal and approval of the Malaysian Cultural Department. At the end, they asked me to add more feathers to my bouncing bosom. Brenna's boobs needed more feathers too. We had too many contours, they just couldn't handle it.

Back in the dressing room we high-fived each other, mocking it as a compliment, but the effect of trying to hide our voluptuousness behind clumps of feathers was pretty tedious and hilarious. The overall aesthetic achieved was something between Big Bird, ostriches on acid, and our great, great grandmother's showgirls. In fact, we took this fully under-exposed opportunity to send photos home to our grandmothers and other Mormon, Muslim, Catholic and Christian relatives who may have been skeptical about what we were actually getting up to out in the far East.

We pulled off a two-hour show that heavily relied on Freddy and Kayla singing, as well as big production numbers with the showgirls not stripping. It was a marathon of a show. Usually we go between group acts, songs, and solo burlesque and variety acts, and I make a point to allow plenty of time for costume and set changes. In this case, we had no solo acts beside songs and tons of extra costume bits to consider. 'Feathers! Feathers! You need more feathers!' This caused us to sweat profusely while running top speed through the hotel's kitchen, changing costumes as we ran, and then scrambling into places in the nick of time.

A number I was surprised got past the censors in the first place turned out to be the biggest crowd pleaser of the night. It was 'Beyond the Sea', our synchronized swimming act, performed to Freddy's live vocals. For whatever reason, maybe because the beach is a big part of the Borneo lifestyle, an exception to the rules was made for this act. We had to keep towels wrapped around our bodies the whole time, as opposed to the pin-up style, 1950's swimsuits we normally wore. While we made our best efforts to keep the towels from coming loose, it wasn't easy. I had to drown Josephine and Star in the fabric sea to readjust themselves, much to the intense amusement of the two young Malaysian boys operating our satin wave, the audience and the rest of the cast. We performed the second half of the number in bellyaching laughter. These slips may account for why it was the audience's favorite.

The Chief Minister of Sarawak, the seventy-four-year-old Pehin Sri Haji Abdul Taib bin Mahmud, was the event's guest of honor.

"You know Ben Stiller, right?" Rupert said to me in the green room. "And you know his movie Zoolander? His mission in that movie is to assassinate the Prime Minister of Malaysia... That's this guy!"

An interesting tidbit of information, indeed. When Pehin Sri Haji Abdul Taib bin Mahmud, or 'Phil' as we called him, arrived, we had to stop the show for a ceremony. He was meant to stay for twenty minutes, but he enjoyed the show so much, he stayed for the whole thing. I was told to take that as the highest of compliments.

There were a thousand people in the audience that evening, making it the largest house we'd ever played to. Half the audience was Muslim. They segregated themselves to one side of the room and the women and men sat at separate tables. They didn't look up from their dinner plates in the direction of the stage once. They didn't clap, barely ate, and didn't talk to each other. The women wore black burkas, a bizarre contrast to the showgirls running between tables in sparkling, Victorian knocking-shop, Moulin Rouge-style Can Can costumes, molting feathers along the way. While that group was resigned to be ambivalent towards us, the other half of the crowd, made up of mostly Chinese, Christian Malays and expats, came up to us afterwards, telling us they loved it and lining up to have their photos taken with The Chinatown Dolls.

The client considered the night a huge success and said that we had gone over sensationally well. The fact that half the people did look up from their plates meant that we'd achieved something, and that some people clapped at the end of the numbers - even better. It's probably safe to say that this was the most interesting gig any of us had ever done. Burlesque in Borneo. The first burlesque show in a Muslim country! Yet another proud first for the history books.

The most rewarding moment for me came after the show. The girls split to the poolside after-party, but I stayed in the dressing room to pack up, enjoying having some alone time, when there was a knock at the door. When I opened it, I was greeted by a bunch of teenage, over-excited hotel staff who had just gotten off work. As they pushed their way into the dressing room, I wondered what was going on. What was this commotion all about? And then, as they touched my hair, staring at me with googly eyes, shoving cameras and bits of paper in face, I realized... The fuss was over me. They swarmed on me like I was the fifth member of The Beatles.

"You are more beautiful than Britney Spears," a tiny girl said, looking up at me.

More beautiful than Britney? I was touched. I guess when your country rejects Beyoncé for being too sexy, that we must look like the next best thing. One boy brazenly asked me to give him a kiss. When I kissed him on the cheek, there were shrieks and yelps. They went nuts. A line formed and pretty soon I was giving away my kisses, and posing for dozens of photographs, even signed a few autographs. I left feeling like I had made their day, but in truth, they really made mine.

By the time I joined the after-party, I expected everyone to be tipsy and carrying on in the pool, but to my surprise, everyone was just standing around. I went straight to the bar, took a double shot of tequila, dropped my dress to my ankles exposing my turquoise bikini, and dove into the deep end, thus beginning the first vacation I'd had in a long, overdue time. I love the silence underwater, like the rest of the world just stops. In just a few strokes, I let myself go, feeling happy to be alive. When I couldn't hold my breath any longer, I floated up to the surface, back into the black night air. Emerging my head above water, I looked around to see everyone silently staring at me. For a second I wondered if I'd committed a major faux pas. Then I saw Kayla and Brenna coming out of the locker room in string bikinis, even smaller than mine. They gleefully jumped into the water and swam over to me. We splashed about, carefree as children playing with abandon.

Pretty soon everyone was stripping down and jumping into the infinity pool. Rupert jumped in fully clothed and did an underwater striptease, as we shouted out the beats of 'The Stripper'. *'Da-da-Da-da-dum, ba-bum-ba-bum...'* The other hotel guests must have thought we were crazy, which was true. But I couldn't help feeling a sense of pride at how this motley crew of misfits had come so far, transforming into a world-class ensemble. From working together so intimately, we'd become closer than friends. It felt like a family.

CHAPTER 29 – Bullshit in a China Shop

"What the fuck is going on?" I shouted, furiously confronting the cast. For the first time practically ever, it was me – not Norman - completely losing my shit. Going ballistic, and Norman telling me to calm down.

No one expected us to be there that night. Beth surprised us by arranging for Norman and me to come back from Borneo four days after the cast. She could see how badly we needed a few days to ourselves, to recharge our batteries and decompress. But all the peaceful mindfulness and blissful enlightenment I'd achieved on vacation had just gone straight out the window. There I was, sat at a table in my own nightclub, expecting to enjoy Chinatown as a guest for the first time, and what do I see on stage? Heidi-Sue badly pretending to be a marionette, getting raped by Rupert.

So again I asked, "What the fuck is going on?" The guilty avoided my eyes, so I continued.

"Three tables just got up and left, and I don't blame them. It's a Saturday night! You opened the show with 'Time for Cocktails'? That's a commercial I wrote for a specific corporate event, not an opening number. Freddy's singing Beatles songs? And then what was that last piece of crap supposed to be?" My hand rubbed my eyes, "It was so bad. I'm speechless."

The running order was posted on the wall. I tore it down, crumpling it into a ball.

"Get ready for '6 Terrific Girls'."

It made me sick to my stomach to think that they'd been performing this miserable, experimental, amateur college shit all week, trying to pass it off as a Chinatown production. I'd worked my butt off honing, tweaking and crafting our shows in order to perfect the formula. To ensure that the Gosney & Kallman brand of entertainment was the best in the world. It didn't happen overnight. And it wasn't to be mangled with. Period. It felt like a slap in the face. Brenna, being the first girl in costume, whispered in my ear while no one was looking that Heidi-Sue was behind it. She had convinced - or bullied - Beth into letting her 'take over' for the week, disregarding my specific instructions.

I'd had enough of Heidi-Sue. She took every chance she got to undermine me or go behind my back to get something her way, and I was over it. Star told me that while we were away Heidi-Sue told Beth that they were all going to quit unless they got raises. There was no choice but for me to confront Beth and try to find out what was really going on.

"She said that the entire cast was going to quit unless we increased their salaries."

"That's bullshit," I said calmly, but matter-of-factly. "I talked to Star and Kayla, Brenna and Freddy, and they were adamant that they had nothing to do with it. It's like that costume business... We were away, she saw an opportunity to manipulate you, and pounced. I can't work with someone like that, we have to let her go." It wasn't only the fact that she was annoying the hell out of me, bringing trouble with her everywhere she went, but performances were suffering as well.

"I can make it work with five girls for the time being, and I have girls lined up ready to take her place. I can train them this week."

Beth took a deep breath and said, "We can't do that Amelia," as if I was dumb to think it would be that easy.

"Why not?"

"Well, there are a few reasons, but mainly because her performance license isn't transferable. So even with understudies, we'd have to buy them each new performance licenses. And she's under contract."

The fact that these Chinese employee contracts existed in the first place was a point of contention between us. And here it was coming back to haunt me, as predicted.

"She could turn around and sue us if we break it," said Beth.

"So, let me get this right," I was doing my best not to lose my temper. "As the director of show and the boss of the cast and crew, you're telling me that I don't reserve the right to fire someone who is not performing or behaving adequately?"

"No, we can fire people Amelia, but not for another six months-"

"Six months? Are you kidding? And stop calling me Amelia; you're speaking down to me like a child. We are partners, Beth. I respect your territory, and I expect you to respect mine."

Whoa. Saying that felt alarming, but good. I'd never stuck up for myself like that before. I stood up a bit taller. Beth became highly interested in a paperclip on her desk, and it was up to me to keep the conversation going if I wanted resolution to the matter.

"So that's it? We're stuck with the old cow? And I suppose she knows that I can't fire her?"

She didn't say anything, except I could see tears forming in her eyes. She was starting to shut down. Then I remembered how this conversation began in the first place.

"At least tell me that you didn't give everyone a raise?"

The words hung in the air like a noose. The longer they hung, the more I could feel a rage growing inside of me as we sat there in a silent square off.

"Not everyone." Meaning just Heidi-Sue.

I got very still. It wasn't about one bad seed anymore. I was staring at a much bigger problem: Having a partner who wasn't making informed, realistic or good decisions in the company's best interest. In a flash, I saw that this was a problem of monumental proportions.

"Where is the extra money coming from? I don't want to be the bad guy on this, of course I'd like to pay everyone more too... Maybe six months from now we'll be in a position to renegotiate, that's always been the plan, but right now with Harley still breathing down our necks, and Goldfish screwing us over... It's impossible. But you know that, right? You've been keeping the books. So tell me. Where's that money going to come from?"

"We'll make it work Amelia. They were going to quit."

"Let them. Call their bluff. I'd rather train a new cast than be blackmailed by some psycho bitch. I can't believe this Beth. I'm so disappointed with your decision on this. You chose her over the good of the company and you got played. *We* got played."

It appeared that there was nothing left to say. Beth wouldn't look at me, so I prepared myself to leave. On my way out the door I turned around and said, "You know this is going to fuck us, right?"

I started to audition new showgirls right away. I may not be able to fire her, but I could start to cut her out of the show. Unfortunately, it was slim pickings for talent in Shanghai. Several of the local dance studios forbid their dancers from working with us, seeing us as the competition. Eventually I invited two girls to come on board whom I trained personally out of our apartment during my free time.

To get their showgirl feet wet, I invited them to start hanging around the club in costume and making cameo appearances onstage on private party nights when I knew there weren't any government spies in the audience. One was a six-foot tall, blonde Amazon from Houston, Texas, and the other, a thin Russian girl with fake tits, who was stunning to look at from a distance, but almost freakishly plastic in a Barbie doll type way up close. For their first performance at Chinatown, I brought them on stage as my assistants in my 'Happy Birthday Baby' act. They held my removed costume pieces as I sauntered around a seated birthday boy, dancing and flirting in my red and gold showgirl costume. Towards the end of the act I smear a chocolate heart on my chest and smother the guy's face in it, right smack between my tits. It's a crowd-pleaser.

The understudies were having the desired effect on the other girls. They rose to the occasion, distinguishing themselves as the reigning queens of the dressing room, and upping their game on stage so the new girls knew who they were competing with. One of the girls was also having an affect on my husband too though. The Texan had approached Norman one night at the club about being a showgirl. He was taken with her blonde hair, tanned skin and big blue eyes, and only mentioned to me that he thought she was 'A very pretty girl', half a dozen times in three sentences. As he said it, I could feel my hackles stand up with a pang of jealousy.

Until that moment, I hadn't really appreciated just how comfortably Norman and I had taken to married life. Recognizing that made my territorial instincts decrease slightly. I knew I could trust him, even if I wasn't so sure I could trust her. Either way, I made a note to self to keep her close to me.

The girls flooded into the dressing room, glowing after the slinky chair dance. It's performed in black lingerie to a slow, smoky version of 'Saint James Infirmary'. Brenna and Josephine were in a heated debate.

"You've only known the guy for what, two weeks?" Brenna said, shaking her head.

"Who?" I asked, being nosey.

"Po-cho," Brenna said in a singsong voice. "Um, okay, just to update you," Brenna continued as Josephine giggled in her chair, "So she met this guy on the beach in Borneo. He's like twenty-years-old…"

"Twenty-two,' Josephine protested.

"Right. Excuse me. He's twenty-two. He's homeless-"

"He lives on the beach-" Brenna rolled her eyes.

"He doesn't speak English, Jo! I mean, come on. And he's already borrowing money off of her, too."

"What? Josephine!"

"I know, but I think he could be the one," she defended, twittering like a teenager.

"Knock-knock." Logan stuck his head around the door, covering his eyes with one hand, always the gentleman. "Just thought you might want to know- Freddy just punched some dude out by the bar."

"What?" This could be bad.

Springing up from my seat, I wrapped my pink silk robe around me to cover the bra and thong I'd been lounging in. I jogged out through the stage door to the front of house in slippers. Across the room, Norman had Freddy up against the wall, a fierce talking to in progress. A meek, baby-faced, Spanish guy stood at the bar with ice in a towel on his eye, the bartender looking after him. I was relieved that the guy wasn't Chinese, as foreigners go to jail for punching locals, even if they'd been punched first.

Star had seen the whole thing. She was standing in her micro-short 'Shanghai Lil' qípáo with arms crossed and a gnarly scowl on her face. I felt a sense of duty to say or do something, but I didn't know what in that situation. Freddy's never hit anyone on our watch before. He knew better than to drink during a show, so the guy must've done something to provoke him.

"Star, what happened?"

"He only talk to me," she said, indicating the scrawny victim.

"She. He. He drink champagne and he say, 'Do I want?' And I say, 'Okay, I want.' And Freddy come and he say, 'You leave her, alone,'" she pointed her finger like a gun. "And he say, 'No, I not leave her, alone.' And then he hit him!" she squeaked in high-pitched distress.

"Are you okay?"

She was far too beautiful for the limits of her experience. Recently, her Shanghainese parents had been pressuring her to quit the club and get married. She was having a hard time standing up to them, despite being in her mid-twenties. I suggested that we could do a special show one night just for her parents. If they could see the club and the quality of shows she was doing, they would have to understand. She wasn't go-go dancing in sweaty discos anymore. She had the best gig in town, and in Chinatown she was a real star. I was willing to do anything I could to help her out since, not only was she my best dancer and one of the club's biggest attractions, she had also become one of my best friends. We didn't always see eye to eye, and I knew that we probably never would because of our different inherited beliefs, but I knew her to have a kind heart, which goes a long ways with me.

My eyes caught sight of someone at the door. Someone who looked a lot like Howie Costello had just walked in. When he made a beeline towards Norman, I couldn't believe it. It was Howie. Norman hadn't told me he was in town. He looked like he'd aged ten years. Unshaven, disheveled, and his greasy hair looked a lot grayer. From the look on Norman's face when he got tapped on the shoulder, I could tell that Howie was the last person in the world he'd expected to see.

Something was wrong with this picture, I sensed. Making my way to the men, I hugged my chest, feeling self-conscious now about being in my pink bathrobe and slippers on the floor of the nightclub.

"Hi Howie," I said, wondering if we were going to hug... He glanced in my direction but didn't stop talking.

"I just wanted to come over here, and I thought, hey! I'll surprise everyone. So I sold my place in LA. Can you believe it? I knew you wouldn't believe it. L.A.'s dead man. Hollywood's over. I'm never going back."

Norman and I looked at each other. He'd gone manic and landed on our doorstep, again. Wickedly amused with himself, he was completely whacked out of his mind. On drugs maybe? He continued to jabber, something about pissing in someone's bed... I couldn't tell if he was serious or joking. Then about how he got on a plane to come here several weeks ago.

"Wait... Weeks? Where've you been staying?" Norman tried, but the guy went right on, as if he physically couldn't stop the words from spewing out of his mouth.

The pieces started to fit together in my head. Then it clicked. I talked over him for Norman's sake, "So you've been here for weeks and you're staying with Heidi-Sue, right? How's that working out for you?"

Norman looked at me like I was nuts. Howie just kept on talking, only making eye-contact when I mentioned Heidi-Sue.

"Norman, I'm going to head backstage to get ready for the finale. I think I need you," I said, offering him an out.

It must have been a full moon, or Mercury was in retrograde, or something like that. I was just glad the night was almost over. Opening the door to the dressing room, I interrupted Kayla and Heidi-Sue in a laughing fit that ended abruptly with my presence.

Changing for the Can Can, I broke the awkward silence, saying "Heidi-Sue, your boyfriend's here." Couldn't resist.

Heidi-Sue's face contorted as it dawned on her what, and who, I was talking about, and then it confirmed my theory that he'd been hiding out at her place. She exchanged a look with Kayla and breathlessly let out a slight, uncomfortable laugh, before taking a long chug of water.

With Kayla's glass of water sat right in front of me, I picked it up muttering, "Sorry, I'm so thirsty, do you mind?"

The glass was on my lips when Kayla shouted, "No don't!" snatching it out of my hand. "It's not water," she confessed bashfully, but it hadn't smelled like alcohol.

"It's okay," said Heidi-Sue. "She could use a few sips."

CHAPTER 30 – Big Trouble in Little Chinatown

Remco's plan officially backfired. When he brought Harley the contractor to the club the night the Gazeeka Box couple got engaged and he saw the club booming, heaving with crowds queuing to get in, he was more than reassured that we would be able to honor our contractual agreement, paying him back in increments over the next 18 months. Things appeared to be going so well that he decided there was no reason we shouldn't pay back the entirety of what we owed his company immediately. If only it was that simple.

Things weren't bad, but we were still paying for the contractor-induced closure after opening night. That and the steady drip-drop stream of bribery demands had made it difficult to stay current with payments to the vendors, the cast and crew, and the landlord. We were doing well, but still catching up. Definitely didn't have the kind of lump sums Harley was after though.

Harley warned that he would 'Take matters into his own hands', if we didn't start payments on his surprise new schedule soon. We had already made him a top priority, managing to have paid him sixty-five percent of the overall figure owed, but Harley claimed to be getting backlash from his employees, who he hadn't paid yet.

"Why hasn't he paid his workers with the money we've already given him?" I asked Norman. "Surely that was the agreement, right?"

"Yup. But now he's shifted all responsibility onto us. Harley's problem of pissed-off, unpaid peasant workers has become our problem."

I don't know why we were surprised that again Harley's word didn't count for anything, and that again he had lied. It's really difficult trying to do business when no one is honest or scrupulous, has any degree of integrity, and only sees things in the shortest of terms, no concept of the bigger, long-term picture. Harley told Remco, who told us, that he 'Wouldn't be able to control what his workers would do', which we took as a serious and direct threat.

With Harley's words hanging over our heads, we asked Remco, our surrogate Chinese partner, for advice. Remco informed us that Harley had family who owned nightclubs. Communist party family who owned nightclubs. He didn't come right out and say it because he didn't have to. When Harley looked at our nightclub he didn't see the show, the dedication, the detail, the unique talent. He was seeing dollar signs. And this 'family' Remco referred to were just the kind of 'close associates' you do not want sniffing around your business.

"If you knew this, why didn't you mention it earlier?" I wanted to know, but no answer was forthcoming.

Remco simply told us that if we wanted to avoid problems with Harley and Harley's 'family', then we needed to honor his request, even though it went against the contract in place. Even though Remco knew that we couldn't afford to 'honor his request'. Remco could afford to though, and the suggestion was brought up that he could cover it for now to get Harley off our backs, consolidating the debt, which we would continue to pay off over the next eighteen months, as planned. It would alleviate the threats and ensure our business got through this bottleneck. But Remco refused without explanation.

All those warnings about Chinese partners that we thought we had avoided were setting off alarm bells in the backs of our minds now. Maybe we were being paranoid, but we were starting to get suspicious of Remco's true motivations, loyalties and interests. Why wouldn't he want to help the business we've all invested in by discharging the threats from some dick-weed if he had the means to? It was curious.

On a Thursday night, Brenna, Josephine and I were sat around the dressing room, gossiping in various stages of undress.

"I tried it once and hated it. It's a good high, but the comedown was awful!"

"What's it called?" I asked.

"Meow Meow," Brenna said.

"Or Plant Food," Josephine added.

This was the first I'd heard of it. The new, hot designer drug, it was said to have similar effects to MDMA and cocaine, but it was cheap and legal. Rupert bought some off the internet and he, Heidi-Sue and several others were getting well stuck into it, nightly. They sprinkled it in water and drank it. The girls said it was why they'd been more bitchy and erratic than usual, inflicting their nasty hangovers on everyone else. It explained a lot actually. I'd noted that they'd been partying hard, not sleeping, and showing up grouchy. Then hours later, they'd be giggling uncontrollably.

"They think they're the characters in *Cabaret*, living the debauched, high-life," Josephine speculated. "But it's becoming most unattractive."

"Yeah, but which one's Liza?" Brenna laughed.

Between the drugs, the hook-ups, and the new girls, I was beginning to feel like we had created some kind of a monster. The troupe was starting to spiral out of control and I had to do something to re-cement us and our intentions back together, before it was too late. We had to move forward, I just wasn't sure how. At first when I thought about what I normally would do, which was throw a party, it seemed a bit ridiculous because every night at Chinatown was a party. That was part of the problem. We needed a team-building activity. A retreat. I broached taking everyone away for a few days with Beth and Norman, but they were both dismissive of the idea, and I knew if I was going to see this through, I'd have to make something happen on my own and with no budget.

That's when I decided to have a good old-fashioned pajama party. Everyone could pile into our living room in PJs and sleeping bags. We would watch old movies, play games, pig out, stay up all night telling funny stories, sleep all day. No drugs. No sex. Just some good clean fun. I wasn't sure how everyone was going to react when I told them at the Thursday night meeting that after Saturday night's show they were all invited to come over to our house for a night or two of pillow fights, food and films. But I didn't care either. It was for their own good, I told myself, believing that our team spirit was still there just under the surface, and worth fighting for. To my pleasure, everyone seemed really excited about the idea, bouncing around in the lead up to the event as if we were a bunch of tweens embarking on our first co-ed sleepover. The plan was working.

After the Saturday night show, I rushed to get my things together so I could beat everyone back to my apartment. I'd set up a big screen to project movies on. We voted to start with *Some Like it Hot*, followed by *Bugsy*.

On my way out, Beth signaled for me to come over. She was talking to a paunchy, permed, average-looking Chinese woman in her mid-forties, wearing a long, pink, cotton dress. I saddled up next to Beth, guessing she wanted to introduce me to the pink lady.

"This is Mrs. Xu. From the Cultural Department," Beth said.

Turns out Mrs. Xu had been there that evening as an undercover spy, following up a complaint by an 'offended' Chinese citizen. The spy showed us incriminating photos on her cellphone of acts that hadn't been registered with the department. Photos that she would be showing to her superiors.

"Who is Amelia Kallman?" the woman asked. Going as white as a sheet I looked to Beth for guidance. She looked like a deer caught in the headlights.

"I'm Amelia Kallman," I said cautiously.

"And your United States of America passport number is 08764242?" she demanded.

"How do you have my passport number?" I wondered aloud.

"The person who complain, they give to me."

My pulse raced. So this was no accident. It was a set-up. And no stranger either. It was personal. Goldfish? My passport details were an unsettling piece of information to dangle in front of the authorities, like someone was trying to get me deported.

"Is there a problem?" I asked.

My primal, survival instincts kicked in as my leg muscles indicated to my brain that they were ready to sprint at any second to the trapdoor backstage if given the signal.

"Yes," she said. "I am very sorry about this, but we have to follow up every complaint. I like what I see. I thought, it is very funny, and I have no problem with what I see myself. Except for that film, I did not like that film."

She was referring to a clip of Sid Vicious singing 'My Way', which we presented in tribute to one of Norman's old mates, Malcolm McLaren, who passed away the previous day. I took some personal satisfaction in the irony of it: We'd offended the Chinese Cultural Department with Sid Vicious' version of 'My Way'. A minor victory on behalf of punks everywhere. People back at The Chelsea Hotel would've been proud.

She gave us until six p.m. the next day to submit videos of every act in our repertoire, and all the words and dialogue had to be transcribed into Chinese too, or else…

It was up to me to break the news to the cast. Not only did we have to come in and perform for the camera on our day off, but this also meant I had to cancel the slumber party. The reactions on their faces broke my heart. I was disappointed too.

"Another time," I assured them.

As I sat in the backseat of the cab coming home that night, the blue lights of the Yan'an Lu reflecting off my face, I could hear the words of Frank Sinatra and Sid Vicious repeat in my head like a mantra:

> *But through it all,*
> *when there was doubt,*
> *I ate it up and spit it out,*
> *I faced it all and I stood tall,*
> *and I did it my way.*

CHAPTER 31 – Chinese Good, Foreigner Bad

With the next payment to Harley coming up, Norman called a meeting with him once more hoping that he could speak to Harley man-to-man and that they could negotiate some new terms and deadlines they could both live with. He had to make Harley understand that if the company neglected to pay the vendors, cast and staff just to appease him, there wouldn't be a product left to gain revenue from, and then everyone would lose.

Norman brought Neptune, his new Chinese assistant hired to replace Goldfish, along to the meeting to interpret, even though he knew perfectly well that Harley's English was probably better than Neptune's. It was all part of the game. I was brought in as well, but as an innocent distraction. My job was to sit in the corner, making sure everyone had tea and lit cigarettes, and laugh at Harley's jokes, smiling the whole time. In part, I was there as décor, because, let's face it, it's a nightclub and having girls around was expected. Also, I was there to play good cop, in case it came to that. My Mandarin wasn't great, but, like Harley, I understood more than I let on.

As soon as the meeting began Harley told Neptune to go buy us coffees from the café around the corner. I offered to go instead, but Harley just looked at me funny and told me to sit back down, and urged Norman to begin.

Norman had mentally prepared for this meeting for days, and spoke clearly, concisely, respectfully and honestly about the facts of the situation, offering suggestions that were realistic and achievable. Watching him in action made me proud, especially because I could see him forcing himself to keep cool. I knew how frustrating this was for him. Harley chain-smoked cigarettes and spit loogies into a cup doubling as an ashtray. It was like I wasn't even in the room, just a fly on the wall. When Norman made his case, a perfectly reasonable and actually extremely generous case, he waited for Harley to respond.

Finally Harley said, "Why you no smile with me and no joke with me? Why you so serious?"

"Harley, you have to understand, this has really been... difficult for me. I've put everything on the line for this. Half a million of my own money, three years of my time, my wife's time and money. We were supposed to open September 17th, but instead we had to close until November, meaning we lost practically two months of revenue, two months of rent and two months of salaries, which has put us two months behind on paying you and everyone else back. Remember how you assured me - looked me in the eye and said 'Yes' the insulation was in the walls? But it wasn't in the walls. And it's because of that... mistake, that's why we're having to have this conversation now. And now I'm trying to offer you a solution that satisfies you, but doesn't put my business at risk. I want to work with you Harley, but you've got to meet me in the middle somewhere."

Harley stared at him for a second and stubbed out his cigarette. Then a switch flipped and he sprang up to his feet, sending his chair crashing back to the ground. Scowling, he got a crazy look in his eye as he shouted violently, pointing his finger in Norman's startled face.

"I don't do bad! I do good. Chinese good. Foreigner bad! You pay me now or I fuck you. You not Chinese, I fuck you bad, you pay me."

Harley looked around the room to make sure it was still only the three of us, before flailing towards the exit. Norman caught up with him in the doorway that was too narrow for them both to squeeze through, forcing Harley to look at him again.

"This is business Harley. I respect you. My apologies," he pressed his palms together and bowed his head. Harley was listening, though his face continued to snarl. "I want to make you happy, I want to make peace. Please, come back and tell me how we can make peace. We want to make harmony."

For a moment, it looked like Norman had gotten through to him and he would sit back down. Then Neptune turned the corner with the coffees and, like he had acquired the audience he longed for, Harley started shouting in Chinese, whipping his hands close to Neptune's face. Caught off guard, Neptune responded in what sounded like an unassuming, natural way, which only enraged Harley more. It was kind of weird to watch a grown man go completely ballistic, throwing a tantrum like a toddler. Harley threw his hands up in the air and stomped off, cursing to himself.

"What did he say?" Norman asked Neptune.

"He said you foreign man don't show love of Chinese way of doing, you disrespect him by saying he did bad, and he wants you to pay him more money."

There was steam coming out of Norman's ears, his face had darkened with anger and I was afraid. He had held back saying what he really thought of Harley and how he really felt this country, and the way they did business like spoiled children.

"So he lost face, is that what you are telling me? It was just the three of us in there! We were speaking English for Christ's sake!"

Norman called Remco's cell. No answer. He sat down for a moment with his head in his hands. I knew better than to try to speak to him. We both sipped our coffees in silence. Finally, he stood up and headed to the office to talk to Beth. I followed, keeping my distance in fear he might explode, but also with the certainty that I was the only person who could keep him from killing someone if he did explode.

As the elevator door on our office floor opened, Norman and I walked out as we caught a glimpse of Harley's fat head steaming past us into the elevator. As the elevator doors shut, Harley held up a piece of paper with a slobbery, taunting grin. What just happened?

Norman *was* going to lose it, or have a heart attack or something, I could see it coming. One of the secretaries buzzed us in and he bolted right up the stairs to where Beth sat at her desk, next to Dougie's vacant office. Her eyes grew big when she saw him.

"What was he doing here?" Norman snapped as he entered.

"Just cal-"

"What was in his hand? Was that a check? Please tell me you did not write him a check Beth, because if you did that would have been the stupidest-" he stopped himself. "Just please tell me you did not just write him a check."

"I will not be talked to this way," Beth said steadily, staring at the papers on her desk.

"I'm sorry," Norman said, taking a deep breath as he pulled a chair up and sat himself down. He stuck a plastered smile on his face and said, "Darling, how are you today? Umm... there was an ugly Chinese man in here a minute ago, named Harley I believe? He left carrying a small piece of paper and had a smile on his face. I was just wondering, since I believe I have a right to know, did you by chance write him a check?"

She had no alternative but to engage with him now that he acknowledged her request to speak civilly, but I could see in the way her eyes zoomed around the room that she was still frightened over what would happen next.

"I did."

Norman stood up, seething, but determined to contain it.

She continued, "He came in here like a crazy person, Norman. He said he was going to come back tonight with a gang and burn the club down if I didn't write him a check right now and-"

"So without speaking to anyone you just cut a check to a mad man who is threatening to destroy our business? Do you know what happens if you bounce a check in this country? You go to jail. But you don't go to jail Beth, I do! Or god forbid, she does."

I had almost forgotten that I wasn't just a fly on the wall, but the thought of going to jail over that little weasel brought me right back to reality.

"It's a post-dated check Norm. He knows not to cash it until I tell him it's okay. He just needed it as insurance, but I had to give it to him to get him out of the office, he was threatening our staff," she appealed.

"He knows, does he? In the meeting we just had he looked me in the eye and told me he was going to fuck me. Starting a paper trail with that guy, something he can now hold over our heads, was a dumb move. Du-umb! His family ranks in the Party, plus he's Triad for fuck sake. He's either so arrogant he thinks he can treat us as he pleases, or he's trying to screw us on purpose so his family, whoever the fuck they really are, can take this place away from us. Don't you get that?"

He turned away from her and put his hand on his heart. My body wanted to rush to him, to make sure he was okay, but it was like I couldn't get the message from my brain to my feet fast enough. He was going to have a stroke any minute now it felt like. Finally, I moved to him and threw myself into his arms. I didn't know what else to do. He was too old and had worked too hard for this shit. He took a breath, giving me a squeeze, before releasing me on a loud exhale, pushing me away again.

"How long do we have then? Anticipating that he doesn't take that check to the bank right now and try to cash it?"

The question froze Beth who looked away from his gaze to ponder that scenario, as if for the first time.

"I told him not to cash it until I tell him to, and he agreed," she said trying to assure him that she had done the right thing, "but it's dated for two weeks from today."

CHAPTER 32 – The Cultural Resolution

The Shanghai World Expo was upon us. A massive trade exposition, it was also an announcement to the world that China's day had come. A giant, blue, toothpaste-squeeze-looking official mascot named Hiabao could be seen on every wall in Shanghai. Written in English, he preached, 'Better City, Better Life'.

"Don't bet on it," Norman would say.

Mexican Hiabao wore a multi-colored poncho and sombrero with a pedo-style mustache. American Hiabao was a cowboy, carrying a lasso and a pistol, a cringe-worthy caricature I found extremely embarrassing. Every Chinese person, all 1.6 billion of them, had been given a free ticket to the Expo to help ensure that they broke all previous World Expo attendance records. So while they boasted that they reached their goal of seventy million attendees, less than six percent of that figure was made up by foreigners. China seemed convinced that their every move was being documented on the front pages of newspapers around the world, but when I mentioned The Expo to people back home, they said they hadn't heard about it. I don't know if that said more about China or the USA.

We were voted Best New Nightclub in Shanghai by the local expat magazine, a major honor that we'd won over a bunch of Chinese-owned clubs. I prayed the award was indeed a blessing, not a curse that would incite jealousy from other nightclub owners.

The government issued a one a.m. curfew across the board on all bars and clubs for the duration of the six-month Expo. Surprisingly, places known for their guangxi, like Shelter and Logo, were shut down with no word about when, or if, they would be allowed to re-open. A multi-national, foreigner owned mega-club, known for its Ponzi scheme financing, just had its Australian accountant sentenced to six years in prison for 'unaccounted for funds'. That verdict had a profound resonance with us foreign business owners. Never before was the potential for bribery to backfire so apparent.

The Expo had given the local authorities an excuse to go nuts. They were coming around again with their hands out saying things like, 'You don't have a license to chop onions. That's a 10,000 kwai fine. But if you pay me 4,000 kwai now, I'll pretend this never happened'. There was no asking why either.

The city was changing and getting more expensive all the time. The cheap streets we used to rely on, like Live Poultry and Fengbang Lu, didn't exist anymore. When we first came to China, I was turned on by the prospect of getting rich so I could raise my status in this world where monetary wealth trumps all and allows people to feel superior over those who have less. But what is that? Is that the American dream? I had learned to get by on very little and in doing so, realized for the first time how rich I already was in the areas of life that truly mattered. As the city had changed, so had I. The girl I was when I came to Shanghai three years earlier, I'd barely recognize today.

I talked Norman into taking the afternoon off to accompany me to a sex shop emporium. He could use a bit of excitement and I needed to buy corsets. After reviewing our submitted material, the Cultural Department came back with their verdict slash punishment. And that was, drum roll please:

No midriffs.

The question of Benny Sideways dressing in women's clothing came up as well, but they ultimately decided that drag was okay… as long as he covered his midriff too. There were Chinese clubs all over this city with girls dancing in far skimpier outfits than ours, and we were trying to run a burlesque club…. And now we can't even show our stomachs? This was starting to get ridiculous.

But I was determined to somehow make it work for us. What else could I do? It was either that or tear my hair out and cry, and no one likes a crying showgirl. I commissioned tight, white latex leotards at the fabric market for The Frug. So what if they were see-thru, they didn't show our midriffs. It was also an opportunity to check out the new sex-shop mall that opened down the street. It seemed a likely place to find corsets, which was the obvious answer to the dilemma. Anyways, Norman and I could use an afternoon excursion away. We worked together everyday, but often it felt like we didn't get to actually see each other and hang. And who knows? Maybe we'd see something we liked that we could look forward to on a day off.

All fantasized titillation vanished as soon as the elevator doors opened. It might have been *the* un-sexiest sex-shop in the world. Motorized sex machines. Gears crunching together. Dicks thrusting in and out of plastic, uninviting, pink pussies. At any sign of interest, an all-too eager old man with no teeth and long, lucky mole-whiskers would flip a switch, demonstrating levels of vibration and encouraging me to touch. It freaked me out. Most disturbing were the blow-up dolls that resembled children and pre-teens. I wish I was making that up, but I'm not. They actually exist. One booth had the dolls lined up in order of height. The smallest one resembled a five-year-old blonde girl with anime eyes and pigtails.

Offended, physically disgusted, and turned-off on so many levels, we decided to get the corsets and get out of there.

The night that the Cultural Department came to follow up on our costume adjustments, they arrived when the doors opened at eight p.m. sharp. They sipped orange juice and ate from complimentary fruit platters and waited for the show to start. I'd written a really sweet show for them, with lots of Chinese comedy and slapstick, something we had perfected by that time. But the Cultural Department only stayed for one number before leaving, implying we had passed the test. So after our first intermission, off came the corsets and I added some more saucy numbers into that night's mix. It was Miss Amelia verse The Communist Party.

By then the club was so popular that we made Friday and Saturday nights private parties. We would only allow people who we knew weren't undercover cops or spies into the club. On these nights we did anything we liked, including several acts that went down to pasties and g-strings. Because our Wednesday and Thursday night shows were covered up and geared towards Chinese audiences, these private party nights became notorious amongst the expat community. As the director and member of the cast, I loved to pace our weekend shows so that by the end, everyone knew they were getting something extra special, and scintillatingly dangerous. Something that wouldn't be filmed or photographed or repeated again. And something we were all in on together, like a true secret society.

CHAPTER 33 – Chinese Fire Drill

The sun had just gone down when I arrived at the club for a Wednesday night show. I got out of the taxi feet first, showing off my new, 3,000 kwai platform, blue velvet stilettos. A local shoe designer had contacted me asking if The Chinatown Dolls would model her latest shoe collection at the pre-opening party for the Salvatore Ferragamo exhibition. All we had to do was show up, look hot, wear the shoes, sip champagne, and as payment she would let us keep the shoes. Being paid in shoes? Hell yeah! Being a showgirl definitely has its perks.

I had every intention of taking my shoes off after showing them to my husband. Secretly, I hoped he'd see me in them and insist on taking me into our back office for a private meeting. With that scenario in mind, I paid the driver and sashayed through the courtyard to the back door. I stopped suddenly when I saw a group of burly local men standing around our air-conditioning shed, blocking the back entrance. The doors to the A.C. unit were broken off the hinges, garbage strewn all over the place, and a fire inside a tin trashcan bellowed black smoke. The men noticed me. There were at least two-dozen. Every one of them turned to stare at me as I tentatively continued walking towards the back entrance of the club, feeling foolish as I towered over the short men in my designer heels.

"Nǐhǎo," I offered quietly, but no one responded.

When I knocked, the door opened an inch. Neptune peered through the hole, saw it was me and quickly let me in, locking the door behind me. Norman stood there with a two-by-four in one hand and his cellphone in the other. Benny and Rupert were right by his shoulders, some kind of queer army preparing for war.

"What's going on?"

"We don't know," Norman said. "These are Harley's workers. They say they're going to burn the club down because that bastard still hasn't paid them yet. I cut a check, another check, specifically for these guys last week, but he's pocketed it again, hasn't he?"

He kept trying to get Remco on the phone, but he wasn't having any luck. Remco could never be reached when we needed him the most. I asked if there was anything I could do.

"Just guard the front door. Make sure no one gets in."

I rushed backstage to change into a pair of leggings and flip-flops. On my way out the door, I turned back around, stopping in the guy's dressing room. Rummaging through Freddy's cubbyhole, I took out his prop gun to offer it to Norman, just in case he wanted to flash it, maybe it would scare them off. When I went back in to find him, Rupert told me Norm had gone outside with the police. Thank god the police were here, I thought. The fake gun went down the back of my leggings and I took post by the front door as instructed.

Outside, I hovered around the corner in sight of Norman and the officers. With Neptune interpreting, Norman addressed the leader of the pack, "Harley's the one who hasn't paid you yet, not us. Take it up with him. Or take us to court, but don't come around here threatening to set fires and destroy our property."

He then asked the police to please arrest and charge the men for destruction of property and trespassing. When Neptune translated this, the police officers smirked in Norman's reddening face that was becoming possessed with vexation, hands gripping into fists. He asked that at the very least, their names be taken down and the incident recorded. The officers told him that he needed to 'make harmony', which was code for 'pay-up'. Their conference moved inside.

The cast, crew and customers were beginning to arrive. Apologetically, I asked them to come back in twenty minutes. I kept poking my head around the corner, wanting to memorize the license plate number on the van the thugs arrived in, in case it came in handy later, as I'd learned to do from watching too many American crime dramas. Not making it out, I took a few steps closer, then crouched down. L47-OUN2. One of the thugs spotted me. He must've understood the thought behind my action. He got his friends to look too. I returned to my post.

Standing there, wishing I had a cigarette to smoke, I heard voices. Then they got louder. The men rushed around the corner in a mob, coming straight at me. They shoved their cellphones in my face, clicking, taking pictures of my terrified expression. I swatted as they swarmed in close, smacking arms away from me, trying to cover my face at the same time. A cellphone smacked the side of my head. They kept coming at me. When my back hit the wall, I remembered the gun. A second later, I held it straight out in front of me with both hands. When I had the courage to look up, I saw them backing off. When the last guy said, 'Fuck you', spit on the ground and flicked his cigarette at me as he turned the corner, I hurried to unlock the front door and get back inside. Slamming it shut behind me, I slid down to the floor. Sitting there in dark silence for several minutes, I tried to understand what just happened. I didn't like that they took my photo, that now they knew my face. I wondered if that was just to harass and provoke me, or if it was so they would know who to come back for later. Who to kidnap and hold for ransom. Or follow home and jump in an alleyway.

Yellow headlights flashed. A white van pulled in. Crawling across the floor, I peeked out the window. I recognized the fat head of Harley as he got out. Someone pulled on the front door to get in and I almost screamed. Through the Judas hole I told them to come back later, before sliding it shut again. About five minutes later, I caught a glimpse of Harley coming out, followed by the police. The laborers piled into their van and drove off.

CHAPTER 34 – Shanghaied

Chops was a well-known photographer from Canada. He could easily be mistaken for one of the Hell's Angels, or a professional wrestler at first glance. With a dyed red beard and muttonchops, he usually sported a bandana and leathers. Despite his hard exterior, he was really a big softy and one of the kindest, coolest people we knew. He had expressed interest in investing in the club, which we were super excited about, especially because it would help us to get Harley out of the picture once and for all. Without the threat of Harley, we were looking at smooth sailing for the future of Chinatown. Chops and his lovely wife invited us over for dinner to discuss things further. Arriving by bicycle with a bottle of wine, Norman was to meet me at their place at five pm.

The previous weekend we threw Chops a birthday party at the club. Norman came up with a photography-theme birthday routine especially for him. This time, Chops was the model sat on stage, while the showgirls took turns powdering him with giant powder puffs, styling, spraying, and applying eye-shadow and blush to his rosy cheeks. We dressed him up as different characters, making a showgirl fuss, before giving Josephine the thumbs up to snap the photo. Norman made a recreation of an old-fashioned box camera that even released a puff of smoke as it snapped. At the end, we presented a mocked-up photo with Chops' face morphed onto a muscle-man's body, and all the showgirls covered him with red lipstick kisses. He was still relishing the memory of it a week later.

When five-thirty rolled around, I called Norman. He told me that he was still at the office and something strange was happening. He whispered into the phone like he was covering his mouth with his hand. One regular size Chinese guy and three giant, local heavies had shown up at the office at five o'clock, he told me. They were demanding 6,000 RMB for a stationary bill that we had no record of. All but two of our office staff had left for the day, there was no money in the office safe, the banks closed at five, and he didn't know how to write a check in Chinese. There was nothing he could do, but they still refused to leave. He wasn't sure what was really going on, whether this was more of Harley's shenanigans, or what.

Another hour passed. I called him again.

One of the guys had laid down on the floor and was now playing dead. His friends called the police, claiming that Norman had punched the guy.

"Did you?" I had to ask.

Norman might not be a large man, but he learned how to fight from his father and wasn't afraid to knock someone out if they deserved it. When we first arrived in Shanghai, there was a drunken guy riding his bike down Urumqi Lu, knocking other cyclists off their bikes for a laugh. When the drunk swerved and was tapped by a car, a shouting match ensued in the middle of the road. An old man in his eighties got out of the passenger seat to try to calm the drunk down, but the drunk proceeded to punch him in the face. The old man's glasses smashed over his eyes, and while there was a whole crowd of people standing around, no one did anything. That's when Norman barreled in, and in one swift move, had the drunk clamped to the pavement under his foot. The crowd applauded and the police thanked him. The funny thing was, by the time he got back to Jubilee Court, our neighborhood spy had already heard the story and congratulated him on being 'The Hero of Urumqi'.

"Honey, I swear on my life, on your life, I didn't touch the guy. I fuckin' wish I had, the little prick. He literally just laid down on the ground." And now the police and an ambulance were there. "I said to the officers, 'Pinch his balls, throw water on him. It's so obvious the guy's faking!' Neptune and one of the office girls are here, and they're telling the truth, that I didn't touch the guy, but the officers are like, 'Ah, but there's only three of you and there's four of them.' They just put him on a stretcher. I think they're going to make me go to the police station. I gotta go."

He hung up.

I sat there on the lid of the toilet wondering what I was supposed to do now. Tell Chops and his missus Norman's not coming because there's been an office invasion and now he's at the police station? Not exactly a scenario I wanted to explain to potential investors.

Norman went to jail. They locked him in a rat-infested cell that stunk from a tin can of someone else's piss in the corner. Mosquitoes and flies swarmed in the stagnate, humid, cigarette smoke air. Norman said it was by far the most disgusting, inhumane conditions he'd ever encountered in a jail, and he'd seen the inside of a few in his day.

A half an hour later, the guy he supposedly beat up came into the station with a doctor's note saying that he'd suffered a severe contusion to the head, caused by a blow. Presenting an 18,000 kwai doctor's bill, he claimed to have had a CAT scan and an MRI. If Norman wanted to get out of prison without being charged, the officer informed him he'd have to pay the bogus stationary bill, plus the bogus doctor's bill, shake hands with the motherfucker, and apologize. *Apologize.*

Norman was freaking out, and I was too. I didn't have 24,000 kwai lying around to bail him out.

Through Neptune, who thankfully stayed to interpret for him, Norman spoke to the officer.

"This is wrong. I didn't touch this guy. I know it, and you know it.... So fine. Let's go legal. I want to call my lawyer and I want to call my embassy."

Neptune and the officer had a lengthy exchange. Finally, Norman was told that if he called a lawyer or his embassy, that would be considered 'An admission of guilt,' and they would be required to keep him there for a minimum of five days, but more likely it would be three weeks. And his bail would be posted at the regular lǎowài rate of 300,000 kwai. Essentially, the officer advised Norman that it was not in his best interest to question what was happening.

We had known of several lǎowài who had been to prison for long periods of time in China. A good friend of ours brother got three weeks after he had been punched in a bar by a Chinese guy, and the Australian punched the guy back. After he got out of jail, he packed up his apartment where he had lived for fifteen years, grabbed his wife and kids, and got on the first plane he could out of the country, quitting his job and leaving his extended family behind. He refused to talk about what it had been like for him in prison, but one can assume it was fairly traumatizing.

Norman was in that cell for over ten hours. Luckily a friend of ours, who in better times, we had bailed out from the clutches of six hookers, came through with the money. I rode my bike home across the Yan'an Lu, way too intoxicated to be on a bicycle, but scared sober. I stopped at JZ Club. I really badly needed a cigarette. Maybe one last drink too, as I wasn't looking forward to returning home alone to an empty apartment. Norman's phone died just after he told me they were finally going to release him. The training police officer they had writing out the paper-work was illiterate, he said, and his superiors kept making him start over again.

It wasn't until I was safely home that my emotions caught up with me. In the corner of the foyer I sank to the floor, unable to hold tears back any longer. I broke down and called Brenna. I had to call someone and she was always so cool. She said she'd come over, but I asked her to just please talk to me. I just needed someone to talk to.

"I don't know how much more of this I can take," I confessed out loud for the first time.

She told me that everything was going to be okay and to just calm down. She eventually got me to a manageable place where I could breath again. After we hung up I ran a bath. The sun was coming up when Norman made it through the door. Clamping my arms around him, I held his body tight, but he said he didn't want to be touched, he just wanted to sleep.

A few days later, Norman told the story to a Chinese who stopped him halfway through saying, 'I tell you the rest of the story'. And he did. Apparently, it's a known scam played on foreigners, with everyone from the ambulance guys and the hospital doctor, to the police officers, in cahoots. Everyone took a cut.

The true zinger, was right before Norman got released, he asked the police chief, "What should I have done differently?"

The chief replied, smiling: "Lie down first."

CHAPTER 35 – The Last Act

At night, the blue light of the Yan'an Lu made people passing in taxicab windows look like Polaroid pictures, captured in time. This journey had become so familiar I could tell where I was with my eyes closed.

It had been a really funny night. Kayla and Star got hooked together by a sequins tangled in someone's fishnet stockings during the new fan dance. They had to do the rest of the act attached at the hip like Siamese twins, trying to wiggle free by rubbing up against each other, which just made it worse. I was in the audience watching them try to improvise the dance saddled together, while trying to keep straight faces. It was hilarious.

The cab dropped me off at the gated back entrance of Jubilee Court. Walking down the lilac scented lane towards our apartment, the moon shone brightly overhead and there was no sound except for the shuffle of my shoes. I anticipated the embrace of my husband with my whole body. The last few weeks had turned me into a clingy and vulnerable child again. I hated to be away from him. Life felt too insecure, too precarious to risk being separated long. I felt this on a primal, survival level.

The latest blow we'd endured was a quote in a long article about us in The Telegraph. We gave the usual appropriate, inoffensive answers, but in an off-the-record conversation after the interview, Norman let it slip that 'It's a fifteen-to-twenty-year-old culture here. It's paranoid and insecure and it makes up for it with bluster. Don't quote me on that', he told the reporter, 'It'll put me out of business'. But he was quoted on it, and that could only be bad.

Shutting the door to the apartment was like shutting the door on China. I was in my own country again. Norman was asleep. I ran a bath and nibbled leftovers in the kitchen, swigging white wine straight from the bottle. I'd been drinking too much recently and I knew it. It was how I was coping with the stress, but obviously I wasn't coping very well. In the bath I touched my body. It wasn't what it used to be. It was surprisingly tighter and more womanly than ever before. I stroked my healing pink scar. I didn't like to look at it. In the bath my breasts were so soft. I made my nipples hard, just because I could. We'd both been too stressed to be intimate lately, and I'd been too busy to find time to look after myself. I couldn't remember the last time I had a hot, wet orgasm, the kind I used to live for. Rubbing my hand between my legs, I closed my eyes, trying to feel pleasure, trying to escape, trying... But it wasn't working. There was no use. I was too tired, and my mind was too far away to even please myself.

The next morning, Norman got up and from the bed I heard his laptop turn on. Within seconds I sat up straight, sensing something wasn't right.

"Baby?" I called.

No response. I don't know why, but something felt wrong. Getting out of bed, I put my long, ivory nightgown on and went into the living room.

"Is everything okay?"

He put a finger up for me to wait, entranced by something on his screen. Maybe there was a natural disaster that happened during the night. Sat on the sofa, I braced myself for something. Or maybe I just had a bad dream and couldn't remember. I'd been having a lot of them lately.

My impatience got the best of me and I asked again, "What's wrong?"

When he turned to me I wondered who died. Then his chest heaved, struggling to get air into his lungs.

Blankly and business-like, he said, "Let me read you this email from Remco...

Dear Norman,

I am sorry to have to do this by e-mail, but I have been traveling for many days. The situation is bad. And it is so bad that I believe we have to take serious actions to counteract a disaster. The issues are mainly related to you personally and that's why this letter is addressed to you. Please read it carefully:

1)   Harley and his subcontractors are warming up for a serious attack on Chinatown. Although I have tried to talk him down, he says that he "Can't take responsibility if anything 'seriously bad' happens to you or Amelia." For some reason Harley keeps on thinking that you are the bad guy and this has

somewhat become personal. I think you have been long enough in China to understand that this is not to be taken lightly. This is the calm before the storm!

2)   He got drunk the night before last at KTV, and yesterday morning he tried to cash three post-dated checks (Written by Beth?) that have bounced. In this country that is considered fraud. According to Chinese criminal law for fraud, it is a five-year minimum prison sentence for 500,000 RMB, so you can imagine what 1.5 million RMB means. You and Amelia are the legal representatives of the company and you are technically personally liable for any authoritative actions against the company. I know quite a few people that have gotten into serious trouble (prison) for much less money. They have now frozen the company's bank accounts and most likely, your personal accounts as well. This is a complete disaster.

3)   A close friend of mine from the Shanghai People's Procurators office has told me that the Xuhui Public Security Bureau is trying to launch a criminal case (drug related?) against Norman Gosney. I don't know who instigated this investigation, how far it has gone, or why it is Xuhui, but if they carry on with this, then you are in very serious trouble, whether there is any merit to the claims or not. The authorities don't want any 'bad apples' during the Expo 'Showtime' for Shanghai, and again, you have become somewhat of a target, though I can't say why.

I think I have described the picture pretty clear here. I have the following comments to all this:

A)   I seriously recommend that Norman and Amelia leave China immediately. I do not, as a friend or partner, want anything unexpected to happen to either of you.

B)   As the government relations-responsible person and 'protector' of Chinatown, I cannot protect Norman and Amelia anymore. The situation has gone too far. I would not want to promise something that I cannot deliver. The situation is out of control and Norman is the main target, with Amelia in danger as well. I cannot guarantee Norman or Amelia's security and safety. Please understand and accept this. Things are heating up behind the scenes, and it could very well run out of control fast.

C)   It was a very clear precondition for me when I joined you on this project that you would not do anything illegal and certainly nothing related to drugs. If there is anything to it, then I am afraid that I can no longer cooperate with you in any way or manner. I have to protect my reputation and what I have built in China over the years through a 100% legal and honest business approach. Drug related crimes are a whole different game in China.

I believe we should try to run the club further and find investors to take it over entirely or partly – and thus try our best to clear the immediate danger – and hopefully get some of our money back, including some return on Norman and Amelia's dollar investment and their huge effort on the project.

I suggest that Norman, Amelia, Dougie and Beth sit down together and decide how to proceed to get Norman and Amelia out of China as soon as possible, as I believe the authorities will be calling for them day after tomorrow, though I cannot make a call as to the specifics. Beth can run the club, and now she will also have to learn to run the show. This may not be ideal, but there is nothing to do about it. I am, as much as anyone, upset it had to end like this!

Yours sincerely, Remco Bredenberg"

"End like this?" The words weren't connecting.

He was kidding, right? We stared at each other, unable to speak words for the longest time. Not able to comprehend. Even when we did start to communicate again, everything sounded trivial next to the intensity of that email.

"Drugs? What's he talking about?" Norman said, shell-shocked. "Where the hell is Xuhui anyways? I've never heard of it...."

At the club, we had nothing to do with drugs. Norman always said it was the cleanest club he'd ever ran. Anywhere else in the world, drug offenses mean possession, but here in the Middle Kingdom, it meant blood tests. Norman would surely test positive for cannabis, his only, and now very occasional, vice.

"And what's that thing about three checks? I know about one, but three?" That was news to me.

"I only knew about one too. I *begged* Beth not to do that. I warned her something bad would happen." We sat in silence for several seconds.

"What is it?" I asked.

"Nothing, it's just that when she first brought it up, the checks I mean, she said Remco had suggested it, but from this..." His hand covered his eyes. None if it was making any sense.

"Fuck Norman. Is this tomorrow? The email said they're coming for us 'Day after tomorrow.' Is this tomorrow? Are we about to get a knock on the-"

I leapt up and bolted to the door, checking the lock, thinking about whether or not we could escape over the balcony if we needed to. Panic set in. Norman tried to call Remco. No answer. Beth. No answer. Dougie. No answer. Remco had copied them in on the email, so they'd also be waking up to it.

"If they've frozen our bank accounts, how can we buy plane tickets?" I said in sudden terror. "Are we wanted Norman? Am I going to Chinese prison for the next five to fifteen years of my life like that email suggests?" I was really starting to freak the fuck out.

"I'm not going back to that prison cell. And you... cannot..." he said, fighting back tears.

I'd never seen him cry before. I, on the other hand, turned to stone. There was no time for feelings. I'd have plenty of time to cry about it later. My fight or flight chemicals kicked in and all I could think was strategy. We had to escape this country, our lives depended on it. It was just a question of how. My first clear thought was *take a shower*. In case they came for me and I was taken away, at least I'd be clean. For some reason that made complete sense at the time.

Finally, Beth called back. She was as hysterical as we were. Apologizing profusely, crying, she too sounded shattered. She said she would come over with Dougie. It would be the first time we'd seen him in almost three months. Thoughts started crossing our minds. Conspiracy theories. The email could be bullshit, a set up, someone trying to push us out. But we're the ones who made it all work. Without us, it would most certainly fall apart. Chops was going to put up the necessary money, but he was investing in us… without us, there would be no deal. And what would happen to the shows? My shows? I didn't want to disappoint our audiences. They trusted me. We'd worked so hard… Our names were all over it… My mind was hemorrhaging.

A knock at the door. My heart flung into my throat. I crept towards the door, then leaned over to look through the peephole. Beth and Dougie. It was a relief. It was odd seeing Dougie. Didn't know whether to hug him or hit him. He'd put weight on and grown a beard to cover a double chin. When he opened the conversation by offering to buy us plane tickets, Norman and I were surprised.

"Where do you want to go?"

A few weeks, or even days ago, that was a question we fantasized about. But now it wasn't nearly as appealing since we were being forced to leave our home, lives, and our baby, Chinatown, possibly forever. We told ourselves we were coming back, because we had to. It was the only way not to break down. We asked Dougie to hold onto our most prized possession, a 3-D portrait of The Chelsea Hotel by the artist David Combs that had been a wedding present from my parents, and he promised to make sure we got it back someday. Beth would come over the following day with a van and move our things into storage.

We hoped that we could get our lawyers on this and it would all blow over and we could return. But in the meantime, we had to get the hell out of Dodge. We decided to go to a friend's villa in Bali, even though it was empty and he wasn't moving in there for another year. It was the closest free place we could think of to stay. Then we had to decide where to go if it didn't blow over. If this was it. My parent's house in Virginia? We couldn't go back to New York, not like this. Go to London and take our chances on Norman's family of friends there? We chose London. It hurt when Dougie said 'one-way'. He booked our flight out for nine a.m. Saturday morning. It was one p.m. on Friday.

That night we brought in extra security and Beth was on the door, ready to push the alarm if the police, or Harley's thugs, tried to come in. If it went off, Norman and I were prepared to exit through the trap door under the stage. We even walked ourselves through the obstacle course once just to be safe. Being backstage was difficult. The girls had a hard time hiding their emotions.

"Amelia, I just want to say thank you," Kayla said. "What you and Norman have done here, it's incredible. And Chinatown, it's the best thing that's ever happened to me."

"Honey, you are one of the sweetest, most talented people I've ever met. I'm so proud of you. Promise me you'll never stop singing," I said.

Her face started to turn pink and her chin quivered.

"No one's ever believed in me like you do," and with that she was sobbing into my cleavage as I stroked her hair and kissed her head, still refusing to let myself cry. I was afraid that if I shed one tear, I'd never be able to stop.

Star came up to us with her lips in a pout. "I feel so sorry for what happens to you and Norman. I feel so bad. I am sorry for the Chinese do this to you. I feel really angry. It is really, really wrong! "

"Shh," I said, and then gave her a hug too, trying not to think about the fact that I may never see her again.

"So Amelia," Brenna interjected, "The pussy: Wax it or shave it? What's the verdict?"

She made me smile. Bless her for knowing me well enough to try to keep this light. I needed that.

"That is the question, isn't it?"

"Wax it," Kayla weighed in.

"Shave it," was Josephine's two cents.

I missed these girls already.

I basically wrote Norman and I out of the show so we could spend most of the evening in the audience, soaking it all in one last time. I stifled back a tsunami of raw, proud, and angry emotions as I watched the show and the crowd lapping it up. Freddy belted out 'New York, New York', dedicating it to us, like at the first show we had done together in Shanghai. It seemed so long ago now. A spontaneous conga line broke out in the audience, snaking between tables. Then we headed backstage for the final act. After all, the show must go on.

I kicked higher than I'd ever kicked in my life. Knee to forehead, whooping in showbiz glee. Norman came out for the number and jumped about on the side of the stage, waving a cane and his bowler. The Acid Ponies flashed the lights like a rave. We waited for the rest of the cast to bow before Norman and I took center stage, hamming it up and dragging out our final bow to a standing ovation. We languished in the praise, knowing undoubtedly that we had earned it.

Walking off our stage that night, a piece of me died. I'd fallen in love with China, given it everything I had, and it had broken my heart.

In the cab headed home, I tried not to think about the things we left behind that I knew somehow we'd never see again: The dozens of costumes I'd carefully constructed by hand, my pastie collection, the King Kong ape suit Norman slaved over, Devon, the framed 'Proprietor's' photo of Norman and me as Bonnie and Clyde... I made room for my Dr. Frankenstein puppet in my suitcase. I couldn't bare to leave him behind. I figured that if I had him, I had some form of bread and butter, even if it was coins tossed in a hat.

We finished packing fifteen minutes before the car picked us up at six a.m. to take us to the airport. We were supposed to leave the country rich, ready for retirement on a beach somewhere, but instead we were leaving with only the cash from the previous night's register and two lonely suitcases. The same ones we arrived with three years earlier.

"If they separate us, don't say anything," Norman said to me at the airport.

I checked my pocket again for the numbers of my embassy and lawyers. The woman behind the counter asked for our passports. She took them, typing into her computer.

"Excuse me," she said, "Please wait here."

She marched towards the back office, clutching our passports in front of her chest. I held my breath.

I thought I was going to be sick.

CHAPTER 36 – China Hearts

A young man in uniform accompanied the woman back to where we stood at the desk. Norman and I looked at each other. My heart was beating rapidly in my chest. The man was looking back and forth between the computer screen and our passports. Then an older man in uniform came over. They spoke in Mandarin, but I couldn't interpret what they were saying. Norman took my hand. We tried to stay calm. The older man looked up at us. He recognized Norman.

"You own nightclub?" the man asked Norman.

"Yes," he replied, gulping.

"China-town! I know! Very, very good club. I have my birthday in your club. I go on stage, with girls," his eyes were shining and he had a big smile across his face, remembering it well. This sudden display of exaltation towards the club and us was unexpected to say the least. Norman smiled back at the guy as he reached to shake his hand. Then the guy recognized me too.

"You! Ah, I know you. Most beautiful dancer in all of Shanghai," he laughed.

He got out his cellphone and asked the girl to take a photograph of him sandwiched between the two of us. Norman and I kept exchanging glances, wondering what was going to happen next. To our relief, the man made sure we were checked into our flight, and then walked with us all the way to the gate. Whatever had come up on the computer screen that had troubled the girl meant nothing now because of our guangxi with her superior. We could hardly believe our luck as the man saw to it that we were looked after, and left us alone to board the flight. So we made it out of the country, and we'll never know exactly what had been the problem that caused her to alert the uniformed man, but we were so thankful that he was the guy on duty that day. What are the odds? I can't tell you... Bless that man.

On the plane I couldn't sleep. Verging on delirium, I'd been awake almost forty hours, surviving on adrenalin. I was beginning to wonder if I would ever sleep again.

In Bali, the driver swerved to avoid cows on the dirt road on the way to the villa. Kids passed on motorbikes in the black night, hair blowing in the wind. Norman chatted away to our driver, which annoyed me greatly for some reason, and then when he swiftly fell back asleep, I was even more irritated at him for leaving me awake, tense and alone. My mind was racing. I still didn't feel safe. My body was shaking, traumatized, and even as I reminded myself to breath, I couldn't stop the feeling that this was it. All I had left in the world now was me, my body, my suitcase and my lover. We had no money, no home, no jobs and suddenly, no future. I thought, *this is what it's like to be zero. This is empty. This is alone.*

The cab pulled up in front of a grey concrete wall. He made a phone call and soon a housekeeper and her daughter came to the driveway to welcome us. I did my best to smile and show my gratitude towards them for staying up to welcome us. They led us behind the wall and through a gate into a villa. To enter we had to walk on a bridge over a pond of koi, into a living space that only had three walls, open to the elements of nature. I tried to remind myself that last week I would've killed to be in a beautiful, private villa in Bali. But this was no vacation.

As soon as the Ayi and child left, Norman took off all his clothes and dove into the pool. He urged me to do the same. When I had no more grumpy excuses, I got in too, staying under water as long as humanly possible. When I floated up, the water lifted me onto my back. Opening my eyes, I was startled by what I saw: Millions of glistening stars in a clear, pitch-black sky, twinkling just for me, like exquisite, shimmering rhinestones.

"Baby, look at all the stars!" I said in wonderment. "I can't believe it. I'd honestly forgotten about stars since Shanghai's too polluted for stars."

"Too polluted for stars... Sounds like a metaphor," he commented.

I closed my eyes and made a wish. I wished that someday everything would be okay again. Someday I would stop being angry and frightened, and maybe even realize that what happened was somehow for the best.

Eighteen hours later we woke up, and it took only seconds for the severity of our situation to shudder back into focus. Norman and I didn't say much, didn't touch much, both trying to stay in a silly state of denial, attuned only to the present because our minds were blown and it hurt to think about both the past and the future. We went around to the landlord's house, an Australian and a Kiwi who lived with their four-year-old son next door.

" 'Ear you've been chucked out of China mate?" The tattooed, topless Kiwi man said with a smile as we entered their villa. "Want a beer?"

We sat down and shared our story in a stream of consciousness, while the expats listened sympathetically. They could see how wrecked we were, still in shock, still in fear. But I never cried. I wondered if something was wrong with me. The couple complained about the problems of being expats in Bali and some of the horror stories they had witnessed, while the Ayi from the night before served us eggs and toast. I was thankful for every bite.

They warned us that the local beach would be crazy that evening, full of drunk tourists and rowdy surfers, but as darkness came, we grew hungry. We couldn't get a motorbike until the next day, so we wandered down to the beach in a daze. The Kiwi was right of course. Not really our scene. For one thing, we were pale as ghosts, making us stick out like sore thumbs, and I felt like a shadow of myself. My defenses had been obliterated, I felt transparent, like people could see right through me. We planned to get food and bring it back to the villa to continue being alone, numb and frozen by the turn of events.

But before that, Norman said, "I need to walk down to the water for a minute. I need to see the ocean."

Reluctantly, I followed him through a rumpus crowd. My teeth grinded with resentment for the carefree people. I couldn't imagine the next time I would feel that way again. Walking past tables full of couples cheerfully eating and drinking, we got to the end of the pier and stared out into the darkness of waves crashing against rocks.

"Norman? Amelia?" a voice with an Italian accent said.

We thought we were imagining things, but then, I couldn't believe my eyes. It was one of Chinatown's frequent customers, our friend, Sergio. Right there in front of me! He threw his arms around us.

"What are the chances, huh?" he said.

He was staying several beaches away and never usually came to that beach. The friends he was with included another exiled Shanghai club owner, who happened to be married to a girl from Norman's hometown of Bristol. What were the chances, indeed.

I'd been desperate for a drink, anything to take the edge off, but we couldn't afford it, so I hadn't bothered bringing it up. When Sergio insisted on getting us drunk, ordering pitchers of margaritas, I couldn't help but crack a smile. I marveled at how fast things can change, at how unpredictable life can be. Norman welcomed a drink too. We even tried to smoke a cigarette, but ended up laughing at ourselves and putting them out after a couple of drags. Later that night, we went back to the villa, amazed at the serendipity of the evening and feeling our faith in the world starting to regenerate.

The next day we got a motorbike and drove back to the beach. We went into a café and ordered granola and coffees, aware that we had to make the little money we had stretch. Norman wandered off again, as he does. I sat in the shade reading a newspaper, when someone grabbed it out of my hands. I sprang to my feet, ready to fight, before I saw who it was:

It was Gage! With his sloppy black hair and chiseled cheekbones, he stood shirtless in red swim trunks looking fiercely tan – right there. Gage! Our first friend in Shanghai. Un-fucking-believable…

"Look what I found!" Norman said, grinning from ear to ear.

Gage had been there three weeks on a tax holiday, with three more weeks to go. As I hugged him, tears bulged in my eyes for the first time since everything happened. I wiped them away quickly with the back of my hand, claiming they were purely made of happiness. Gage was staying several beaches over and, he too, never came to that beach. He just happened to jog in that direction that day, and Norman just happened to go out at the exact same time. They literally ran into each other. As I stood there with my arms around Gage's waist, trying to grasp the odds of this sequence of coincidences, the saying, 'Everything happens for a reason' came to mind. It was like a message from the universe trying to tell me that things were going to be okay.

We had an email from Beth saying the police came looking for us at the office that Saturday afternoon. They told our secretary they'd been to our home that morning. I imagined them smashing down the door to find our vacated apartment and the smell of incense still wafting through the air. We must've just missed them. The police raided the club that night, setting up security at all exits so no one could leave. They stopped the show, searched the dressing rooms, and turned the place upside down. They asked every employee and customer to form a line against the wall. One by one, they verified everyone's home address and legality on a laptop. It had only been recently, in the past few months or so, the police had upgraded to computers.

Beth said they kept asking where we were, threatening to put her in jail if they found out she was lying and we really were in the country, not away 'for health reasons'. She mentioned that she thought it might be possible for me to return, but Norman definitely couldn't risk it. We were advised by her, Remco and our lawyers not to speak to anyone – press, investors, employees – as to prevent our story from negatively influencing the future of the club.

After a week of absorbing the blow in Bali, we flew to London. Norman's old friends, on hearing he was coming unexpectedly, jokingly placed bets on whether or not he was on the run with Interpol on his tail. We were met at Heathrow and wholeheartedly taken into the bosom of a family by Norman's dear old friends and their two gorgeous, precocious little girls. I woke up early on the first morning there to give the kids hugs before they went to school. They were full of questions.

"Is it true that in China they eat cats? What about dogs? So, like, if I lived there, and I brought Ozzy with me, would they eat him?"

Her little brown eyes looked very concerned about the prospect of someone eating her cat. I debated whether or not I should tell her the truth – yes, the Chinese eats cats and dogs – but for the child's sake I told her that I was sure no one would eat Ozzy, and that I'd tell her everything she wanted to know about China when she got home from school.

I stood on a street corner in Nottinghill for ten minutes as if I was in a new world. The faces passing by me were a mix of colors, dressed in a range of fashions, and speaking English. It was strange, but I was in awe. Maybe I wasn't back in my own country, but I knew I was in a safe country. A country with freedom. Another thing that amazed me was the ability to drink water from the tap. What a luxury. I stood in front of the sink filling up my glass and drinking until I thought I would burst.

It took us two weeks of decompression to get our health back on track. When you're in China for as long as we were, you get used to the pollution and stop noticing it, but I remember walking outside at Heathrow airport and noticing the difference. And London's considered a city of high pollution, but it has got nothing on Shanghai. Norman's blood pressure had been through the roof. Our doctor friend said he was lucky he hadn't had a stroke or a heart attack.

Slowly, I began to feel safe again. I made Norman swear to me a hundred times that no one could hurt us now. We couldn't be extradited back to China or imprisoned indefinitely. We would never get our money back either though, and that was something we just had to accept. All things considered, they could have our money. It was a small price to pay for our lives and freedom.

In a quiet, meditative moment, alone in the guestroom of our mate's house, I laid upon the white bedspread of a four-poster bed. With French doors opened onto an English garden, first edition Banksy's hung on the walls, next to Warhol's Mao prints, slightly ironic. It was then that I made a decision: Even if I could, I'd never go back to China. It was too unsafe, and I just had to be thankful that I'd made it out okay.

Letting the decision sink in, I went outside and laid down on a hammock under the clear night sky and took a deep breath of the fragrant summer air. I looked up to thank my lucky stars for getting me this far and giving me another chance to start again. Letting go of our China lives and dream wasn't a choice we wanted to make, but our hands were forced. We'd given it everything we had, put ourselves on the line, and the dragon defeated us. Our China hearts were broken. It would be easy for some naysayers to call us failures, but I couldn't be more proud of what we achieved, for we successfully achieved the impossible. Even if it didn't last forever, nothing ever does, and we still had the time of our lives. And in doing so, we made a lot of people genuinely happy. No one can take that away from us.

While it may not have turned out the way we planned, how many things in life actually do? I couldn't admit it before, but now I can: A part of me felt relief. Relief that the daily struggles, the lies I told myself to make it all okay, and the constant fear that something like what happened, would happen, was finally over.

Even though in some respects we lost everything, I was more thankful than ever. I had my freedom. I got my voice back to say and express how I feel and what I think, a privilege that I'd never fully appreciated the richness of before. Sure, I might have lost material possessions, but the stories I gained, the friendships I made, and the lessons I learned, are invaluable. My future will only benefit from the journeys of my past.

And of course, there was one other thing that made everything worth it and everything okay, and that's Norman.

"There you are," he said approaching me, "I was wondering where you'd gone, I missed you."

"Get in here," I said, making room for him on the hammock.

As we swung back and forth, I nuzzled my head onto his shoulder. I told him my decision about not going back to China.

"Even if I could, I've decided I won't. I couldn't go back without you. We're in this thing together, you and me."

He kissed my forehead and held me close. I realized then that for the first time in my life, the blank pages of my future didn't frighten me anymore. If I could live through this, I was tough enough to survive anything. It's like the secret of life I wrote on that pack of Camel Lights: *We have to keep moving forward.*

And I would.

ABOUT THE AUTHOR

Originally from Fairfax, Virginia, Amelia Kallman grew up entertaining audiences on many of Washington D.C.'s most prestigious stages. She studied acting at Marymount Manhattan College, and Shakespeare at the British American Dramatics Academy. While living in the penthouse of The Chelsea Hotel with her partner, Norman Gosney, they ran an illegal speakeasy, The Blushing Diamond, before moving to Shanghai to open China's first burlesque nightclub, the award-winning Gosney & Kallman's Chinatown.

Since relocating to the UK, she has lectured at Cambridge University, written a graphic novel, scripts for television, and articles for an array of online publications. She currently lives in London with her husband and dog.

Made in the USA
Middletown, DE
20 August 2015